W9-AGO-546

EVERYMAN,
I WILL GO WITH THEE
AND BE THY GUIDE,
IN THY MOST NEED
TO GO BY THY SIDE

EVERYMAN'S LIBRARY
POCKET POETS

WHITMAN

·······················

POEMS

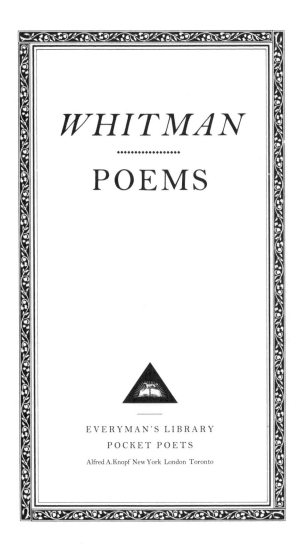

EVERYMAN'S LIBRARY
POCKET POETS

Alfred A. Knopf New York London Toronto

THIS IS A BORZOI BOOK
PUBLISHED BY ALFRED A. KNOPF

This selection by Peter Washington first published in
Everyman's Library, 1994
Copyright © 1994 by Everyman's Library

Fourteenth printing (US)

All rights reserved. Published in the United States by Alfred A. Knopf,
a division of Random House, Inc., New York, and in Canada by Random
House of Canada Limited, Toronto. Distributed by Random House, Inc.,
New York. Published in the United Kingdom by Everyman's Library,
Northburgh House, 10 Northburgh Street, London EC1V 0AT.
Distributed by Random House (UK) Ltd.

US website: www.randomhouse.com/everymans

ISBN 978-0-679-43632-4 (US)
978-1-85715-715-4 (UK)

A CIP catalogue record for this book is available from the British Library

Typography by Peter B. Willberg
Typeset in the UK by AccComputing, North Barrow, Somerset
Printed and bound in Germany by GGP Media GmbH, Pössneck

CONTENTS

Birds of Passage   11
These Carols   11
Poets to Come   12
I Hear America Singing   13
Native Moments   14
When I Heard at the Close of the Day   15
Roots and Leaves Themselves Alone   17
I Saw in Louisiana a Live-Oak Growing   18
To a Stranger   19
A Glimpse   20
Among the Multitude   21
Youth, Day, Old Age and Night   22
A Noiseless Patient Spider   23
Me Imperturbe   24
My Picture-Gallery   25
A Hand-Mirror   26
Halcyon Days   27
The Dalliance of the Eagles   28
Old Salt Kossabone   29
A Twilight Song   30
The Runner   32
Perfections .. ..:   32
O Tan-Faced Prairie-Boy   33
Sometimes with One I Love   33
Whoever You Are Holding Me Now in Hand   34

A Sight in Camp in the Daybreak Gray and Dim .. 37
Vigil Strange I Kept on the Field One Night 39
An Army Corps on the March 42
Cavalry Crossing a Ford 43
The Wound-Dresser 44
Reconciliation 49
As I Lay with my Head in your Lap Camerado 50
Crossing Brooklyn Ferry 51
There Was a Child Went Forth 62
Starting from Paumanok 66
Song of Myself 87
The Sleepers 186
Passage to India 203
Out of the Cradle Endlessly Rocking 219
When Lilacs Last in the Dooryard Bloom'd 230
Whispers of Heavenly Death 244
So Long! 245

Index of First Lines 251

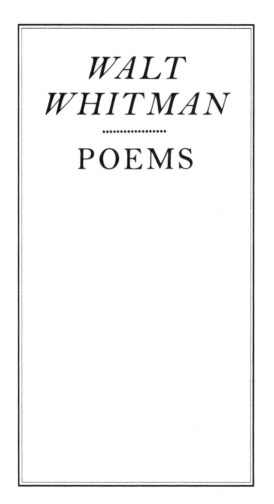

WALT WHITMAN

POEMS

BIRDS OF PASSAGE
Song of the Universal

I

Come said the Muse,
Sing me a song no poet yet has chanted,
Sing me the universal.

In this broad earth of ours,
Amid the measureless grossness and the slag,
Enclosed and safe within its central heart,
Nestles the seed perfection.

By every life a share or more or less,
None born but it is born, conceal'd or unconceal'd the
     seed is waiting.

1874

THESE CAROLS

These carols sung to cheer my passage through the
     world I see,
For completion I dedicate to the Invisible World.

1871

11

POETS TO COME

Poets to come! orators, singers, musicians to come!
Not to-day is to justify me and answer what I am for,
But you, a new brood, native, athletic, continental,
    greater than before known,
Arouse! for you must justify me.

I myself but write one or two indicative words for the
    future,
I but advance a moment only to wheel and hurry back
    in the darkness.

I am a man who, sauntering along without fully
    stopping, turns a casual look upon you and then
    averts his face,
Leaving it to you to prove and define it,
Expecting the main things from you.

1860

I HEAR AMERICA SINGING

I hear America singing, the varied carols I hear,
Those of mechanics, each one singing his as it should
    be blithe and strong,
The carpenter singing his as he measures his plank or
    beam,
The mason singing his as he makes ready for work, or
    leaves off work,
The boatman singing what belongs to him in his boat,
    the deck-hand singing on the steamboat deck,
The shoemaker singing as he sits on his bench, the
    hatter singing as he stands,
The wood-cutter's song, the ploughboy's on his way in
    the morning, or at noon intermission or at
    sundown,
The delicious singing of the mother, or of the young
    wife at work, or of the girl sewing or washing,
Each singing what belongs to him or her and to none
    else,
The day what belongs to the day – at night the party of
    young fellows, robust, friendly,
Singing with open mouths their strong melodious
    songs.

1860

NATIVE MOMENTS

Native moments – when you come upon me – ah you
    are here now,
Give me now libidinous joys only,
Give me the drench of my passions, give me life coarse
    and rank,
To-day I go consort with Nature's darlings, to-night
    too,
I am for those who believe in loose delights, I share the
    midnight orgies of young men,
I dance with the dancers and drink with the drinkers,
The echoes ring with our indecent calls, I pick out
    some low person for my dearest friend,
He shall be lawless, rude, illiterate, he shall be one
    condemn'd by others for deeds done,
I will play a part no longer, why should I exile myself
    from my companions?
O you shunn'd persons, I at least do not shun you,
I come forthwith in your midst, I will be your poet,
I will be more to you than to any of the rest.

1860

WHEN I HEARD AT THE CLOSE OF
THE DAY

When I heard at the close of the day how my name had
      been receiv'd with plaudits in the capitol, still it
      was not a happy night for me that follow'd,
And else when I carous'd, or when my plans were
      accomplish'd, still I was not happy,
But the day when I rose at dawn from the bed of
      perfect health, refresh'd, singing, inhaling the ripe
      breath of autumn,
When I saw the full moon in the west grow pale and
      disappear in the morning light,
When I wander'd alone over the beach, and undressing
      bathed, laughing with the cool waters, and saw
      the sun rise,
And when I thought how my dear friend my lover was
      on his way coming, O then I was happy,
O then each breath tasted sweeter, and all that day my
      food nourish'd me more, and the beautiful day
      pass'd well,
And the next came with equal joy, and with the next at
      evening came my friend,
And that night while all was still I heard the waters
      roll slowly continually up the shores,
I heard the hissing rustle of the liquid and sands as
      directed to me whispering to congratulate me,

For the one I love most lay sleeping by me under the
    same cover in the cool night,
In the stillness in the autumn moonbeams his face was
    inclined toward me,
And his arm lay lightly around my breast – and that
    night I was happy.

1860

ROOTS AND LEAVES THEMSELVES ALONE

Roots and leaves themselves alone are these,
Scents brought to men and women from the wild
    woods and pond-side,
Breast-sorrel and pinks of love, fingers that wind
    around tighter than vines,
Gushes from the throats of birds hid in the foliage of
    trees as the sun is risen,
Breezes of land and love set from living shores to you
    on the living sea, to you O sailors!
Frost-mellow'd berries and Third-month twigs offer'd
    fresh to young persons wandering out in the fields
    when the winter breaks up,
Love-buds put before you and within you whoever you
    are,
Buds to be unfolded on the old terms,
If you bring the warmth of the sun to them they will
    open and bring form, color, perfume, to you,
If you become the aliment and the wet they will
    become flowers, fruits, tall branches and trees.

1860

I SAW IN LOUISIANA A LIVE-OAK GROWING

I saw in Louisiana a live-oak growing,
All alone stood it and the moss hung down from the
      branches,
Without any companion it grew there uttering joyous
      leaves of dark green,
And its look, rude, unbending, lusty, made me think of
      myself,
But I wonder'd how it could utter joyous leaves
      standing alone there without its friend near, for I
      knew I could not,
And I broke off a twig with a certain number of leaves
      upon it, and twined around it a little moss,
And brought it away, and I have placed it in sight in
      my room,
It is not needed to remind me as of my own dear
      friends,
(For I believe lately I think of little else than of them,)
Yet it remains to me a curious token, it makes me think
      of manly love;
For all that, and though the live-oak glistens there in
      Louisiana solitary in a wide flat space,
Uttering joyous leaves all its life without a friend a
      lover near,
I know very well I could not.

1860

TO A STRANGER

Passing stranger! you do not know how longingly I
    look upon you,
You must be he I was seeking, or she I was seeking, (it
    comes to me as of a dream,)
I have somewhere surely lived a life of joy with you,
All is recall'd as we flit by each other, fluid, affectionate,
    chaste, matured,
You grew up with me, were a boy with me or a girl
    with me,
I ate with you and slept with you, your body has
    become not yours only nor left my body mine
    only,
You give me the pleasure of your eyes, face, flesh, as we
    pass, you take of my beard, breast, hands, in
    return,
I am not to speak to you, I am to think of you when I
    sit alone or wake at night alone,
I am to wait, I do not doubt I am to meet you again,
I am to see to it that I do not lose you.

1860

A GLIMPSE

A glimpse through an interstice caught,
Of a crowd of workmen and drivers in a bar-room
      around the stove late of a winter night, and I
      unremark'd seated in a corner,
Of a youth who loves me and whom I love, silently
      approaching and seating himself near, that he
      may hold me by the hand,
A long while amid the noises of coming and going, of
      drinking and oath and smutty jest,
There we two, content, happy in being together,
      speaking little, perhaps not a word.

1860

AMONG THE MULTITUDE

Among the men and women the multitude,
I perceive one picking me out by secret and divine
  signs,
Acknowledging none else, not parent, wife, husband,
  brother, child, any nearer than I am,
Some are baffled, but that one is not – that one knows
  me.

Ah lover and perfect equal,
I meant that you should discover me so by faint
  indirections,
And I when I meet you mean to discover you by the
  like in you.

1860

YOUTH, DAY, OLD AGE AND NIGHT

Youth, large, lusty, loving – youth full of grace, force,
    fascination,
Do you know that Old Age may come after you with
    equal grace, force, fascination?

Day full-blown and splendid – day of the immense sun,
    action, ambition, laughter,
The Night follows close with millions of suns, and
    sleep and restoring darkness.

1881

A NOISELESS PATIENT SPIDER

A noiseless patient spider,
I mark'd where on a little promontory it stood isolated,
Mark'd how to explore the vacant vast surrounding,
It launch'd forth filament, filament, filament, out of
    itself,
Ever unreeling them, ever tirelessly speeding them.

And you O my soul where you stand,
Surrounded, detached, in measureless oceans of space,
Ceaselessly musing, venturing, throwing, seeking the
    spheres to connect them,
Till the bridge you will need be form'd, till the ductile
    anchor hold,
Till the gossamer thread you fling catch somewhere,
    O my soul.

1868

ME IMPERTURBE

Me imperturbe, standing at ease in Nature,
Master of all or mistress of all, aplomb in the midst of
    irrational things,
Imbued as they, passive, receptive, silent as they,
Finding my occupation, poverty, notoriety, foibles,
    crimes, less important than I thought,
Me toward the Mexican sea, or in the Mannahatta or
    the Tennessee, or far north or inland,
A river man, or a man of the woods, or of any farm-life
    of these States or of the coast, or the lakes or
    Kanada,
Me wherever my life is lived, O to be self-balanced for
    contingencies,
To confront night, storms, hunger, ridicule, accidents,
    rebuffs, as the trees and animals do.

1860

MY PICTURE-GALLERY

In a little house keep I pictures suspended, it is not a
    fix'd house,
It is round, it is only a few inches from one side to the
    other;
Yet behold, it has room for all the shows of the world,
    all memories!
Here the tableaus of life, and here the groupings of
    death;
Here, do you know this? this is cicerone himself,
With finger rais'd he points to the prodigal pictures.

1880

A HAND-MIRROR

Hold it up sternly – see this it sends back, (who is it?
    is it you?)
Outside fair costume, within ashes and filth,
No more a flashing eye, no more a sonorous voice or
    springy step,
Now some slave's eye, voice, hands, step,
A drunkard's breath, unwholesome eater's face,
    venerealee's flesh,
Lungs rotting away piecemeal, stomach sour and
    cankerous,
Joints rheumatic, bowels clogged with abomination,
Blood circulating dark and poisonous streams,
Words babble, hearing and touch callous,
No brain, no heart left, no magnetism of sex;
Such from one look in this looking-glass ere you go
    hence,
Such a result so soon – and from such a beginning!

1860

HALCYON DAYS

Not from successful love alone,
Nor wealth, nor honor'd middle age, nor victories of
      politics or war;
But as life wanes, and all the turbulent passions calm,
As gorgeous, vapory, silent hues cover the evening
      sky,
As softness, fulness, rest, suffuse the frame, like fresher,
      balmier air,
As the days take on a mellower light, and the apple at
      last hangs really finish'd and indolent-ripe on the
      tree,
Then for the teeming quietest, happiest days of all!
The brooding and blissful halcyon days!

1888

THE DALLIANCE OF THE EAGLES

Skirting the river road, (my forenoon walk, my rest,)
Skyward in air a sudden muffled sound, the dalliance of
    the eagles,
The rushing amorous contact high in space together,
The clinching interlocking claws, a living, fierce,
    gyrating wheel,
Four beating wings, two beaks, a swirling mass tight
    grappling,
In tumbling turning clustering loops, straight
    downward falling,
Till o'er the river pois'd, the twain yet one, a moment's
    lull,
A motionless still balance in the air, then parting,
    talons loosing,
Upward again on slow-firm pinions slanting, their
    separate diverse flight,
She hers, he his, pursuing.

1880

OLD SALT KOSSABONE

Far back, related on my mother's side,
Old Salt Kossabone, I'll tell you how he died:
(Had been a sailor all his life – was nearly 90 – lived
    with his married grandchild, Jenny;
House on a hill, with view of bay at hand, and distant
    cape, and stretch to open sea;)
The last of afternoons, the evening hours, for many a
    year his regular custom,
In his great arm chair by the window seated,
(Sometimes, indeed, through half the day,)
Watching the coming, going of the vessels, he mutters
    to himself – And now the close of all:
One struggling outbound brig, one day, baffled for
    long – cross-tides and much wrong going,
At last at nightfall strikes the breeze aright, her whole
    luck veering,
And swiftly bending round the cape, the darkness
    proudly entering, cleaving, as he watches,
'She's free – she's on her destination' – these the last
    words – when Jenny came, he sat there dead,
Dutch Kossabone, Old Salt, related on my mother's
    side, far back.

1888

A TWILIGHT SONG

As I sit in twilight late alone by the flickering oak
    flame,
Musing on long-pass'd war-scenes – of the countless
    buried unknown soldiers,
Of the vacant names, as unindented air's and sea's – the
    unreturn'd,
The brief truce after battle, with grim burial-squads,
    and the deep-fill'd trenches,
Of gather'd dead from all America, North, South, East,
    West, whence they came up,
From wooded Maine, New-England's farms, from
    fertile Pennsylvania, Illinois, Ohio,
From the measureless West, Virginia, the South, the
    Carolinas, Texas,
(Even here in my room-shadows and half-lights in the
    noiseless flickering flames,
Again I see the stalwart ranks on-filing, rising – I hear
    the rhythmic tramp of the armies;)
You million unwrit names all, all – you dark bequest
    from all the war,

A special verse for you – a flash of duty long neglected
    – your mystic roll strangely gather'd here,
Each name recall'd by me from out the darkness and
    death's ashes,
Henceforth to be, deep, deep within my heart
    recording, for many a future year,
Your mystic roll entire of unknown names, or North or
    South,
Embalm'd with love in this twilight song.

1890

THE RUNNER

On a flat road runs the well-train'd runner,
He is lean and sinewy with muscular legs,
He is thinly clothed, he leans forward as he runs,
With lightly closed fists and arms partially rais'd.

1867

PERFECTIONS

Only themselves understand themselves and the like of
    themselves,
As souls only understand souls.

1860

O TAN-FACED PRAIRIE-BOY

O tan-faced prairie-boy,
Before you came to camp came many a welcome gift,
Praises and presents came and nourishing food, till at
    last among the recruits,
You came, taciturn, with nothing to give – we but
    look'd on each other,
When lo! more than all the gifts of the world you gave
    me.

1865

SOMETIMES WITH ONE I LOVE

Sometimes with one I love I fill myself with rage for
    fear I effuse unreturn'd love,
But now I think there is no unreturn'd love, the pay is
    certain one way or another,
(I loved a certain person ardently and my love was not
    return'd,
Yet out of that I have written these songs.)

1860

WHOEVER YOU ARE HOLDING ME NOW IN HAND

Whoever you are holding me now in hand,
Without one thing all will be useless,
I give you fair warning before you attempt me further,
I am not what you supposed, but far different.

Who is he that would become my follower?
Who would sign himself a candidate for my affections?

The way is suspicious, the result uncertain, perhaps
     destructive,
You would have to give up all else, I alone would
     expect to be your sole and exclusive standard,
Your novitiate would even then be long and
     exhausting,
The whole past theory of your life and all conformity
     to the lives around you would have to be
     abandon'd,
Therefore release me now before troubling yourself
     any further, let go your hand from my shoulders,
Put me down and depart on your way.

Or else by stealth in some wood for trial,
Or back of a rock in the open air,
(For in any roof'd room of a house I emerge not, nor in
company,
And in libraries I lie as one dumb, a gawk, or unborn,
or dead,)
But just possibly with you on a high hill, first watching
lest any person for miles around approach
unawares,
Or possibly with you sailing at sea, or on the beach of
the sea or some quiet island,
Here to put your lips upon mine I permit you,
With the comrade's long-dwelling kiss or the new
husband's kiss,
For I am the new husband and I am the comrade.

Or if you will, thrusting me beneath your clothing,
Where I may feel the throbs of your heart or rest upon
your hip,
Carry me when you go forth over land or sea;
For thus merely touching you is enough, is best,
And thus touching you would I silently sleep and be
carried eternally.

But these leaves conning you con at peril,
For these leaves and me you will not understand,
They will elude you at first and still more afterward, I
   will certainly elude you,
Even while you should think you had unquestionably
   caught me, behold!
Already you see I have escaped from you.

For it is not for what I have put into it that I have
   written this book,
Nor is it by reading it you will acquire it,
Nor do those know me best who admire me and
   vauntingly praise me,
Nor will the candidates for my love (unless at most a
   very few) prove victorious,
Nor will my poems do good only, they will do just as
   much evil, perhaps more,
For all is useless without that which you may guess at
   many times and not hit, that which I hinted at;
Therefore release me and depart on your way.

1860

A SIGHT IN CAMP IN THE DAYBREAK GRAY AND DIM

A sight in camp in the daybreak gray and dim,
As from my tent I emerge so early sleepless,
As slow I walk in the cool fresh air the path near by the
     hospital tent,
Three forms I see on stretchers lying, brought out
     there untended lying,
Over each the blanket spread, ample brownish woolen
     blanket,
Gray and heavy blanket, folding, covering all.

Curious I halt and silent stand,
Then with light fingers I from the face of the nearest
    the first just lift the blanket;
Who are you elderly man so gaunt and grim, with
    well-gray'd hair, and flesh all sunken about the
    eyes?
Who are you my dear comrade?
Then to the second I step – and who are you my child
    and darling?
Who are you sweet boy with cheeks yet blooming?
Then to the third – a face nor child nor old, very calm,
    as of beautiful yellow-white ivory;
Young man I think I know you – I think this face is the
    face of the Christ himself,
Dead and divine and brother of all, and here again he
    lies.

1865

VIGIL STRANGE I KEPT ON THE FIELD ONE NIGHT

Vigil strange I kept on the field one night;
When you my son and my comrade dropt at my side
     that day,
One look I but gave which your dear eyes return'd with
     a look I shall never forget,
One touch of your hand to mine O boy, reach'd up as
     you lay on the ground,
Then onward I sped in the battle, the even-contested
     battle,
Till late in the night reliev'd to the place at last again I
     made my way,
Found you in death so cold dear comrade, found your
     body son of responding kisses, (never again on
     earth responding,)
Bared your face in the starlight, curious the scene, cool
     blew the moderate night-wind,
Long there and then in vigil I stood, dimly around me
     the battle-field spreading,

Vigil wondrous and vigil sweet there in the fragrant
    silent night,
But not a tear fell, not even a long-drawn sigh, long,
    long I gazed,
Then on the earth partially reclining sat by your side
    leaning my chin in my hands,
Passing sweet hours, immortal and mystic hours with
    you dearest comrade – not a tear, not a word,
Vigil of silence, love and death, vigil for you my son
    and my soldier,
As onward silently stars aloft, eastward new ones
    upward stole,
Vigil final for you brave boy, (I could not save you,
    swift was your death,
I faithfully loved you and cared for you living, I think
    we shall surely meet again,)
Till at latest lingering of the night, indeed just as the
    dawn appear'd,
My comrade I wrapt in his blanket, envelop'd well his
    form,

Folded the blanket well, tucking it carefully over head
     and carefully under feet,
And there and then and bathed by the rising sun, my
     son in his grave, in his rude-dug grave I
     deposited,
Ending my vigil strange with that, vigil of night and
     battle-field dim,
Vigil for boy of responding kisses, (never again on
     earth responding,)
Vigil for comrade swiftly slain, vigil I never forget,
     how as day brighten'd,
I rose from the chill ground and folded my soldier well
     in his blanket,
And buried him where he fell.

1865

AN ARMY CORPS ON THE MARCH

With its cloud of skirmishers in advance,
With now the sound of a single shot snapping like a
      whip, and now an irregular volley,
The swarming ranks press on and on, the dense
      brigades press on,
Glittering dimly, toiling under the sun – the dust-
      cover'd men,
In columns rise and fall to the undulations of the
      ground,
With artillery interspers'd – the wheels rumble, the
      horses sweat,
As the army corps advances.

1865–6

CAVALRY CROSSING A FORD

A line in long array where they wind betwixt green
    islands,
They take a serpentine course, their arms flash in the
    sun – hark to the musical clank,
Behold the silvery river, in it the splashing horses
    loitering stop to drink,
Behold the brown-faced men, each group, each person
    a picture, the negligent rest on the saddles,
Some emerge on the opposite bank, others are just
    entering the ford – while,
Scarlet and blue and snowy white,
The guidon flags flutter gayly in the wind.

1865

THE WOUND-DRESSER

I

An old man bending I come among new faces,
Years looking backward resuming in answer to
    children,
Come tell us old man, as from young men and maidens
    that love me,
(Arous'd and angry, I'd thought to beat the alarum, and
    urge relentless war,
But soon my fingers fail'd me, my face droop'd and I
    resign'd myself,
To sit by the wounded and soothe them, or silently
    watch the dead;)
Years hence of these scenes, of these furious passions,
    these chances,
Of unsurpass'd heroes, (was one side so brave? the
    other was equally brave;)
Now be witness again, paint the mightiest armies of
    earth,
Of those armies so rapid so wondrous what saw you to
    tell us?
What stays with you latest and deepest? of curious
    panics,
Of hard-fought engagements or sieges tremendous
    what deepest remains?

II

O maidens and young men I love and that love me,
What you ask of my days those the strangest and
    sudden your talking recalls,
Soldiers alert I arrive after a long march cover'd with
    sweat and dust,
In the nick of time I come, plunge in the fight, loudly
    shout in the rush of successful charge,
Enter the captur'd works – yet lo, like a swift-running
    river they fade,
Pass and are gone they fade – I dwell not on soldiers'
    perils or soldiers' joys,
(Both I remember well – many the hardships, few the
    joys, yet I was content.)

But in silence, in dreams' projections,
While the world of gain and appearance and mirth
    goes on,
So soon what is over forgotten, and waves wash the
    imprints off the sand,
With hinged knees returning I enter the doors, (while
    for you up there,
Whoever you are, follow without noise and be of
    strong heart.)

Bearing the bandages, water and sponge,
Straight and swift to my wounded I go,
Where they lie on the ground after the battle brought
in,
Where their priceless blood reddens the grass the
ground,
Or to the rows of the hospital tent, or under the roof'd
hospital,
To the long rows of cots up and down each side I
return,
To each and all one after another I draw near, not one
do I miss,
An attendant follows holding a tray, he carries a refuse
pail,
Soon to be fill'd with clotted rags and blood, emptied,
and fill'd again.

I onward go, I stop,
With hinged knees and steady hand to dress wounds,
I am firm with each, the pangs are sharp yet
unavoidable,
One turns to me his appealing eyes – poor boy! I never
knew you,
Yet I think I could not refuse this moment to die for
you, if that would save you.

III

On, on I go, (open doors of time! open hospital doors!)
The crush'd head I dress, (poor crazed hand tear not
　　the bandage away,)
The neck of the cavalry-man with the bullet through
　　and through I examine,
Hard the breathing rattles, quite glazed already the
　　eye, yet life struggles hard,
(Come sweet death! be persuaded O beautiful death!
In mercy come quickly.)

From the stump of the arm, the amputated hand,
I undo the clotted lint, remove the slough, wash off the
　　matter and blood,
Back on his pillow the soldier bends with curv'd neck
　　and side-falling head,
His eyes are closed, his face is pale, he dares not look on
　　the bloody stump,
And has not yet look'd on it.

I dress a wound in the side, deep, deep,
But a day or two more, for see the frame all wasted and
　　sinking,
And the yellow-blue countenance see.

I dress the perforated shoulder, the foot with the
    bullet-wound,
Cleanse the one with a gnawing and putrid gangrene,
    so sickening, so offensive,
While the attendant stands behind aside me holding
    the tray and pail.

I am faithful, I do not give out,
The fractur'd thigh, the knee, the wound in the
    abdomen,
These and more I dress with impassive hand, (yet deep
    in my breast a fire, a burning flame.)

IV

Thus in silence in dreams' projections,
Returning, resuming, I thread my way through the
    hospitals,
The hurt and wounded I pacify with soothing hand,
I sit by the restless all the dark night, some are so
    young,
Some suffer so much, I recall the experience sweet and
    sad,
(Many a soldier's loving arms about this neck have
    cross'd and rested,
Many a soldier's kiss dwells on these bearded lips.)

1865

RECONCILIATION

Word over all, beautiful as the sky,
Beautiful that war and all its deeds of carnage must in
      time be utterly lost,
That the hands of the sisters Death and Night
      incessantly softly wash again, and ever again, this
      soil'd world;
For my enemý is dead, a man divine as myself is dead,
I look where he lies white-faced and still in the coffin –
      I draw near,
Bend down and touch lightly with my lips the white
      face in the coffin.

1865–6

AS I LAY WITH MY HEAD IN YOUR LAP CAMERADO

As I lay with my head in your lap camerado,
The confession I made I resume, what I said to you and
      the open air I resume,
I know I am restless and make others so,
I know my words are weapons full of danger, full of
      death,
For I confront peace, security and all the settled laws,
      to unsettle them,
I am more resolute because all have denied me than I
      could ever have been had all accepted me,
I heed not and have never heeded either experience,
      cautions, majorities, nor ridicule,
And the threat of what is call'd hell is little or nothing
      to me,
And the lure of what is call'd heaven is little or nothing
      to me;
Dear camerado! I confess I have urged you onward
      with me, and still urge you, without the least idea
      what is our destination,
Or whether we shall be victorious, or utterly quell'd
      and defeated.

1865–6

CROSSING BROOKLYN FERRY

I

Flood-tide below me! I see you face to face!
Clouds of the west – sun there half an hour high – I see
    you also face to face.

Crowds of men and women attired in the usual
    costumes, how curious you are to me!
On the ferry-boats the hundreds and hundreds that
    cross, returning home, are more curious to me
    than you suppose,
And you that shall cross from shore to shore years
    hence are more to me, and more in my
    meditations, than you might suppose.

II

The impalpable sustenance of me from all things at all
    hours of the day,
The simple, compact, well-join'd scheme, myself
    disintegrated, every one disintegrated yet part of
    the scheme,
The similitudes of the past and those of the future,
The glories strung like beads on my smallest sights
    and hearings, on the walk in the street and the
    passage over the river,

The current rushing so swiftly and swimming with me
    far away,
The others that are to follow me, the ties between me
    and them,
The certainty of others, the life, love, sight, hearing of
    others.

Others will enter the gates of the ferry and cross from
    shore to shore,
Others will watch the run of the flood-tide,
Others will see the shipping of Manhattan north and
    west, and the heights of Brooklyn to the south
    and east,
Others will see the islands large and small;
Fifty years hence, others will see them as they cross,
    the sun half an hour high,
A hundred years hence, or ever so many hundred years
    hence, others will see them,
Will enjoy the sunset, the pouring-in of the flood-tide,
    the falling-back to the sea of the ebb-tide.

III

It avails not, time nor place – distance avails not,
I am with you, you men and women of a generation, or
    ever so many generations hence,
Just as you feel when you look on the river and sky, so I
    felt,

Just as any of you is one of a living crowd, I was one of
      a crowd,
Just as you are refresh'd by the gladness of the river
        and the bright flow, I was refresh'd,
Just as you stand and lean on the rail, yet hurry with
        the swift current, I stood yet was hurried,
Just as you look on the numberless masts of ships and
        the thick-stemm'd pipes of steamboats, I look'd.
I too many and many a time cross'd the river of old,
Watched the Twelfth-month sea-gulls, saw them high
        in the air floating with motionless wings,
        oscillating their bodies,
Saw how the glistening yellow lit up parts of their
        bodies and left the rest in strong shadow,
Saw the slow-wheeling circles and the gradual edging
        towards the south,
Saw the reflection of the summer sky in the water,
Had my eyes dazzled by the shimmering track of
        beams,
Look'd at the fine centrifugal spokes of light round the
        shape of my head in the sunlit water,
Look'd on the haze on the hills southward and
        south-westward,
Look'd on the vapor as it flew in fleeces tinged with
        violet,
Look'd toward the lower bay to notice the vessels
        arriving,

Saw their approach, saw aboard those that were near
    me,
Saw the white sails of schooners and sloops, saw the
    ships at anchor,
The sailors at work in the rigging or out astride the
    spars,
The round masts, the swinging motion of the hulls, the
    slender serpentine pennants,
The large and small steamers in motion, the pilots in
    their pilot-houses,
The white wake left by the passage, the quick
    tremulous whirl of the wheels,
The flags of all nations, the falling of them at sunset,
The scallop-edged waves in the twilight, the ladled
    cups, the frolicsome crests and glistening,
The stretch afar growing dimmer and dimmer, the
    gray walls of the granite storehouses by the
    docks,
On the river the shadowy group, the big steam-tug
    closely flank'd on each side by the barges, the hay-
    boat, the belated lighter,
On the neighboring shore the fires from the foundry
    chimneys burning high and glaringly into the
    night,
Casting their flicker of black contrasted with wild red
    and yellow light over the tops of houses, and
    down into the clefts of streets.

IV

These and all else were to me the same as they are to
　　you,
I loved well those cities, loved well the stately and
　　rapid river,
The men and women I saw were all near to me,
Others the same – others who look back on me because
　　I look'd forward to them,
(The time will come, though I stop here to-day and
　　to-night.)

V

What is it then between us?
What is the count of the scores or hundreds of years
　　between us?

Whatever it is, it avails not – distance avails not, and
　　place avails not,
I too lived, Brooklyn of ample hills was mine,
I too walk'd the streets of Manhattan island, and
　　bathed in the waters around it,
I too felt the curious abrupt questionings stir within
　　me,
In the day among crowds of people sometimes they
　　came upon me,
In my walks home late at night or as I lay in my bed
　　they came upon me,

I too had been struck from the float forever held in
      solution,
I too had receiv'd identity by my body,
That I was I knew was of my body, and what I should
      be I knew I should be of my body.

VI

It is not upon you alone the dark patches fall,
The dark threw its patches down upon me also,
The best I had done seem'd to me blank and suspicious,
My great thoughts as I supposed them, were they not
      in reality meagre?
Nor is it you alone who know what it is to be evil,
I am he who knew what it was to be evil,
I too knitted the old knot of contrariety,
Blabb'd, blush'd, resented, lied, stole, grudg'd,
Had guile, anger, lust, hot wishes I dared not speak,
Was wayward, vain, greedy, shallow, sly, cowardly,
      malignant,
The wolf, the snake, the hog, not wanting in me,
The cheating look, the frivolous word, the adulterous
      wish, not wanting,
Refusals, hates, postponements, meanness, laziness,
      none of these wanting,
Was one with the rest, the days and haps of the rest,
Was call'd by my nighest name by clear loud voices of
      young men as they saw me approaching or
      passing,

Felt their arms on my neck as I stood, or the negligent
      leaning of their flesh against me as I sat,
Saw many I loved in the street or ferry-boat or public
      assembly, yet never told them a word,
Lived the same life with the rest, the same old
      laughing, gnawing, sleeping,
Play'd the part that still looks back on the actor or
      actress,
The same old role, the role that is what we make it, as
      great as we like,
Or as small as we like, or both great and small.

VII

Closer yet I approach you,
What thought you have of me now, I had as much of
      you – I laid in my stores in advance,
I consider'd long and seriously of you before you were
      born.

Who was to know what should come home to me?
Who knows but I am enjoying this?
Who knows, for all the distance, but I am as good as
      looking at you now, for all you cannot see me?

VIII

Ah, what can ever be more stately and admirable to me
    than mast-hemm'd Manhattan?

River and sunset and scallop-edg'd waves of
    flood-tide?

The sea-gulls oscillating their bodies, the hay-boat in
    the twilight, and the belated lighter?

What gods can exceed these that clasp me by the hand,
    and with voices I love call me promptly and
    loudly by my nighest name as I approach?

What is more subtle than this which ties me to the
    woman or man that looks in my face?

Which fuses me into you now, and pours my meaning
    into you?

We understand then do we not?

What I promis'd without mentioning it, have you not
    accepted?

What the study could not teach – what the preaching
    could not accomplish is accomplish'd, is it not?

IX

Flow on, river! flow with the flood-tide, and ebb with
    the ebb-tide!

Frolic on, crested and scallop-edg'd waves!

Gorgeous clouds of the sunset! drench with your
    splendor me, or the men and women generations
    after me!

Cross from shore to shore, countless crowds of
  passengers!
Stand up, tall masts of Mannahatta! stand up, beautiful
  hills of Brooklyn!
Throb, baffled and curious brain! throw out questions
  and answers!
Suspend here and everywhere, eternal float of solution!
Gaze, loving and thirsting eyes, in the house or street
  or public assembly!
Sound out, voices of young men! loudly and musically
  call me by my nighest name!
Live, old life! play the part that looks back on the actor
  or actress!
Play the old role, the role that is great or small
  according as one makes it!
Consider, you who peruse me, whether I may not in
  unknown ways be looking upon you;
Be firm, rail over the river, to support those who lean
  idly, yet haste with the hasting current;
Fly on, sea-birds! fly sideways, or wheel in large circles
  high in the air;
Receive the summer sky, you water, and faithfully hold
  it till all downcast eyes have time to take it from
  you!
Diverge, fine spokes of light, from the shape of my
  head, or any one's head, in the sunlit water!

Come on, ships from the lower bay! pass up or down,
      white-sail'd schooners, sloops, lighters!
Flaunt away, flags of all nations! be duly lower'd at
      sunset!
Burn high your fires, foundry chimneys! cast black
      shadows at nightfall! cast red and yellow light
      over the tops of the houses!
Appearances, now or henceforth, indicate what you
      are,
You necessary film, continue to envelop the soul,
About my body for me, and your body for you, be hung
      our divinest aromas,
Thrive, cities – bring your freight, bring your shows,
      ample and sufficient rivers,
Expand, being than which none else is perhaps more
      spiritual,
Keep your places, objects than which none else is more
      lasting.

You have waited, you always wait, you dumb, beautiful
      ministers
We receive you with free sense at last, and are insatiate
      henceforward,
Not you any more shall be able to foil us, or withhold
      yourselves from us,
We use you, and do not cast you aside – we plant you
      permanently within us,

We fathom you not – we love you – there is perfection
      in you also,
You furnish your parts toward eternity,
Great or small, you furnish your parts toward the soul.

1856

THERE WAS A CHILD WENT FORTH

There was a child went forth every day,
And the first object he look'd upon, that object he
      became,
And that object became part of him for the day or a
      certain part of the day,
Or for many years or stretching cycles of years.

The early lilacs became part of this child,
And grass and white and red morning-glories, and
      white and red clover, and the song of the
      phœbe-bird,
And the Third-month lambs and the sow's pink-faint
      litter, and the mare's foal and the cow's calf,
And the noisy brood of the barnyard or by the mire of
      the pondside,
And the fish suspending themselves so curiously below
      there, and the beautiful curious liquid,
And the water-plants with their graceful flat heads, all
      became part of him.

The field-sprouts of Fourth-month and Fifth-month
became part of him,
Winter-grain sprouts and those of the light-yellow
corn, and the esculent roots of the garden,
And the apple-trees cover'd with blossoms and the
fruit afterward, and wood-berries, and the
commonest weeds by the road,
And the old drunkard staggering home from the
outhouse of the tavern whence he had lately risen,
And the schoolmistress that pass'd on her way to the
school,
And the friendly boys that pass'd, and the quarrelsome
boys,
And the tidy and fresh-cheek'd girls, and the barefoot
negro boy and girl,
And all the changes of city and country wherever he
went.

His own parents, he that had father'd him and she that
had conceiv'd him in her womb and birth'd him,
They gave this child more of themselves than that,
They gave him afterward every day, they became part
of him.

The mother at home quietly placing the dishes on the
supper-table,
The mother with mild words, clean her cap and gown,
a wholesome odor falling off her person and
clothes as she walks by,
The father, strong, self-sufficient, manly, mean,
anger'd, unjust,
The blow, the quick loud word, the tight bargain, the
crafty lure,
The family usages, the language, the company, the
furniture, the yearning and swelling heart,
Affection that will not be gainsay'd, the sense of what
is real, the thought if after all it should prove
unreal,
The doubts of day-time and the doubts of night-time,
the curious whether and how,
Whether that which appears so is so, or is it all flashes
and specks?
Men and women crowding fast in the streets, if they
are not flashes and specks what are they?
The streets themselves and the façades of houses, and
goods in the windows,
Vehicles, teams, the heavy-plank'd wharves, the huge
crossing at the ferries,
The village on the highland seen from afar at sunset,
the river between,

Shadows, aureola and mist, the light falling on roofs
and gables of white or brown two miles off,
The schooner near by sleepily dropping down the tide,
the little boat slack-tow'd astern,
The hurrying tumbling waves, quick-broken crests,
slapping,
The strata of color'd clouds, the long bar of maroon-
tint away solitary by itself, the spread of purity it
lies motionless in,
The horizon's edge, the flying sea-crow, the fragrance
of salt marsh and shore mud,
These became part of that child who went forth every
day, and who now goes, and will always go forth
every day.

1855

STARTING FROM PAUMANOK

I

Starting from fish-shape Paumanok where I was born,
Well-begotten, and rais'd by a perfect mother,
After roaming many lands, lover of populous
    pavements,
Dweller in Mannahatta my city, or on southern
    savannas,
Or a soldier camp'd or carrying my knapsack and gun,
    or a miner in California,
Or rude in my home in Dakota's woods, my diet meat,
    my drink from the spring,
Or withdrawn to muse and meditate in some deep
    recess,
Far from the clank of crowds intervals passing rapt
    and happy,
Aware of the fresh free giver the flowing Missouri,
    aware of mighty Niagara,
Aware of the buffalo herds grazing the plains, the
    hirsute and strong-breasted bull,
Of earth, rocks, Fifth-month flowers experienced,
    stars, rain, snow, my amaze,
Having studied the mocking-bird's tones and the flight
    of the mountain-hawk,
And heard at dawn the unrivall'd one, the hermit
    thrush from the swamp-cedars,
Solitary, singing in the West, I strike up for a New
    World.

II

Victory, union, faith, identity, time,
The indissoluble compacts, riches, mystery,
Eternal progress, the kosmos, and the modern reports.

This then is life,
Here is what has come to the surface after so many
      throes and convulsions.

How curious! how real!
Underfoot the divine soil, overhead the sun.

See revolving the globe,
The ancestor-continents away group'd together,
The present and future continents north and south, ·
      with the isthmus between.

See, vast trackless spaces,
As in a dream they change, they swiftly fill,
Countless masses debouch upon them,
They are now cover'd with the foremost people, arts,
      institutions, known.

See, projected through time,
For me an audience interminable.

With firm and regular step they wend, they never stop,
Successions of men, Americanos, a hundred millions,
One generation playing its part and passing on,
Another generation playing its part and passing on in
    its turn,
With faces turn'd sideways or backward towards me to
    listen,
With eyes retrospective towards me.

III

Americanos! conquerors! marches humanitarian!
Foremost! century marches! Libertad! masses!
For you a programme of chants.

Chants of the prairies,
Chants of the long-running Mississippi, and down to
    the Mexican sea,
Chants of Ohio, Indiana, Illinois, Iowa, Wisconsin and
    Minnesota,
Chants going forth from the centre from Kansas, and
    thence equidistant,
Shooting in pulses of fire ceaseless to vivify all.

IV

Take my leaves America, take them South and take
    them North,
Make welcome for them everywhere, for they are your
    own offspring,
Surround them East and West, for they would
    surround you,
And you precedents, connect lovingly with them, for
    they connect lovingly with you.

I conn'd old times,
I sat studying at the feet of the great masters,
Now if eligible O that the great masters might return
    and study me.

In the name of these States shall I scorn the antique?
Why these are the children of the antique to justify it.

V

Dead poets, philosophs, priests,
Martyrs, artists, inventors, governments long since,
Language-shapers on other shores,
Nations once powerful, now reduced, withdrawn, or
    desolate,
I dare not proceed till I respectfully credit what you
    have left wafted hither,

I have perused it, own it is admirable, (moving awhile
    among it,)
Think nothing can ever be greater, nothing can ever
    deserve more than it deserves,
Regarding it all intently a long while, then dismissing
    it,
I stand in my place with my own day here.

Here lands female and male,
Here the heir-ship and heiress-ship of the world, here
    the flame of materials,
Here spirituality the translatress, the openly-avow'd,
The ever-tending, the finalè of visible forms,
The satisfier, after due long-waiting now advancing,
Yes here comes my mistress the soul.

VI

The soul,
Forever and forever – longer than soil is brown and
    solid – longer than water ebbs and flows.

I will make the poems of materials, for I think they are
    to be the most spiritual poems,
And I will make the poems of my body and of
    mortality,
For I think I shall then supply myself with the poems
    of my soul and of immortality.

I will make a song for these States that no one State
      may under any circumstances be subjected to
      another State,
And I will make a song that there shall be comity by
      day and by night between all the States, and
      between any two of them,
And I will make a song for the ears of the President,
      full of weapons with menacing points,
And behind the weapons countless dissatisfied faces;
And a song make I of the One form'd out of all,
The fang'd and glittering One whose head is over all,
Resolute warlike One including and over all,
(However high the head of any else that head is over
      all.)

I will acknowledge contemporary lands,
I will trail the whole geography of the globe and salute
      courteously every city large and small,
And employments! I will put in my poems that with
      you is heroism upon land and sea,
And I will report all heroism from an American point
      of view.

I will sing the song of companionship,
I will show what alone must finally compact these,
I believe these are to found their own ideal of manly
      love, indicating it in me,

I will therefore let flame from me the burning fires that
    were threatening to consume me,
I will lift what has too long kept down those
    smouldering fires,
I will give them complete abandonment,
I will write the evangel-poem of comrades and of love,
For who but I should understand love with all its
    sorrow and joy?
And who but I should be the poet of comrades?

VII

I am the credulous man of qualities, ages, races,
I advance from the people in their own spirit,
Here is what sings unrestricted faith.

Omnes! omnes! let others ignore what they may,
I make the poem of evil also, I commemorate that part
    also,
I am myself just as much evil as good, and my nation is
    – and I say there is in fact no evil,
(Or if there is I say it is just as important to you, to the
    land or to me, as anything else.)

I too, following many and follow'd by many,
　　inaugurate a religion, I descend into the arena,
(It may be I am destin'd to utter the loudest cries there,
　　the winner's pealing shouts,
Who knows? they may rise from me yet, and soar
　　above every thing.)

Each is not for its own sake,
I say the whole earth and all the stars in the sky are for
　　religion's sake.

I say no man has ever yet been half devout enough,
None has ever yet adored or worship'd half enough,
None has begun to think how divine he himself is, and
　　how certain the future is.

I say that the real and permanent grandeur of these
　　States must be their religion,
Otherwise there is no real and permanent grandeur;
(Nor character nor life worthy the name without
　　religion,
Nor land nor man or woman without religion.)

VIII

What are you doing young man?
Are you so earnest, so given up to literature, science,
　　art, amours?

These ostensible realities, politics, points?
Your ambition or business whatever it may be?

It is well – against such I say not a word, I am their
        poet also,
But behold! such swiftly subside, burnt up for
        religion's sake,
For not all matter is fuel to heat, impalpable flame, the
        essential life of the earth,
Any more than such are to religion.

IX

What do you seek so pensive and silent?
What do you need camerado?
Dear son do you think it is love?
Listen dear son – listen America, daughter or son,
It is a painful thing to love a man or woman to excess,
        and yet it satisfies, it is great,
But there is something else very great, it makes the
        whole coincide,
It, magnificent, beyond materials, with continuous
        hands sweeps and provides for all.

X

Know you, solely to drop in the earth the germs of a
        greater religion,
The following chants each for its kind I sing.

My comrade!
For you to share with me two greatnesses, and a third
  one rising inclusive and more resplendent,
The greatness of Love and Democracy, and the
  greatness of Religion.
Melange mine own, the unseen and the seen,
Mysterious ocean where the streams empty,
Prophetic spirit of materials shifting and flickering
  around me,
Living beings, identities now doubtless near us in the
  air that we know not of,
Contact daily and hourly that will not release me,
These selecting, these in hints demanded of me.

Not he with a daily kiss onward from childhood kissing
  me,
Has winded and twisted around me that which holds
  me to him,
Any more than I am held to the heavens and all the
  spiritual world,
After what they have done to me, suggesting themes.

O such themes – equalities! O divine average!
Warblings under the sun, usher'd as now, or at noon,
  or setting,
Strains musical flowing through ages, now reaching
  hither,

I take to your reckless and composite chords, add to
　　them, and cheerfully pass them forward.

XI

As I have walk'd in Alabama my morning walk,
I have seen where the she-bird the mocking-bird sat on
　　her nest in the briers hatching her brood.

I have seen the he-bird also,
I have paus'd to hear him near at hand inflating his
　　throat and joyfully singing.

And while I paus'd it came to me that what he really
　　sang for was not there only,
Nor for his mate nor himself only, nor all sent back by·
　　the echoes,
But subtle, clandestine, away beyond,
A charge transmitted and gift occult for those being
　　born.

XII

Democracy! near at hand to you a throat is now
　　inflating itself and joyfully singing.

Ma femme! for the brood beyond us and of us,
For those who belong here and those to come,
I exultant to be ready for them will now shake out
    carols stronger and haughtier than have ever yet
    been heard upon earth.

I will make the songs of passions to give them their
    way,
And your songs outlaw'd offenders, for I scan you with
    kindred eyes, and carry you with me the same as
    any.

I will make the true poem of riches,
To earn for the body and the mind whatever adheres
    and goes forward and is not dropt by death;
I will effuse egotism and show it underlying all, and I
    will be the bard of personality,
And I will show of male and female that either is but
    the equal of the other,
And sexual organs and acts! do you concentrate in me,
    for I am determin'd to tell you with courageous
    clear voice to prove you illustrious,
And I will show that there is no imperfection in the
    present, and can be none in the future,
And I will show that whatever happens to anybody it
    may be turn'd to beautiful results,

And I will show that nothing can happen more
    beautiful than death,
And I will thread a thread through my poems that time
    and events are compact,
And that all the things of the universe are perfect
    miracles, each as profound as any.

I will not make poems with reference to parts,
But I will make poems, songs, thoughts, with reference
    to ensemble,
And I will not sing with reference to a day, but with
    reference to all days,
And I will not make a poem nor the least part of a
    poem but has reference to the soul,
Because having look'd at the objects of the universe, I
    find there is no one nor any particle of one but has
    reference to the soul.

XIII

Was somebody asking to see the soul?
See, your own shape and countenance, persons,
    substances, beasts, the trees, the running rivers,
    the rocks and sands.

All hold spiritual joys and afterwards loosen them;
How can the real body ever die and be buried?

Of your real body and any man's or woman's real body,
Item for item it will elude the hands of the corpse-
    cleaners and pass to fitting spheres,
Carrying what has accrued to it from the moment of
    birth to the moment of death.

Not the types set up by the printer return their
    impression, the meaning, the main concern,
Any more than a man's substance and life or a woman's
    substance and life return in the body and the soul,
Indifferently before death and after death.

Behold, the body includes and is the meaning, the main
    concern, and includes and is the soul;
Whoever you are, how superb and how divine is your
    body, or any part of it!

XIV

Whoever you are, to you endless announcements!

Daughter of the lands did you wait for your poet?
Did you wait for one with a flowing mouth and
    indicative hand?
Toward the male of the States, and toward the female
    of the States,
Exulting words, words to Democracy's lands.

Interlinked, food-yielding lands!
Land of coal and iron! land of gold! land of cotton,
    sugar, rice!
Land of wheat, beef, pork! land of wool and hemp! land
    of the apple and the grape!
Land of the pastoral plains, the grass-fields of the
    world! land of those sweet-air'd interminable
    plateaus!
Land of the herd, the garden, the healthy house of
    adobie!
Lands where the north-west Columbia winds, and
    where the south-west Colorado winds!
Land of the eastern Chesapeake! land of the Delaware!
Land of Ontario, Erie, Huron, Michigan!
Land of the Old Thirteen! Massachusetts land! land of
    Vermont and Connecticut!
Land of the ocean shores! land of sierras and peaks!
Land of boatmen and sailors! fishermen's land!
Inextricable lands! the clutch'd together! the
    passionate ones!
The side by side! the elder and younger brothers! the
    bony-limb'd!
The great women's land! the feminine! the experienced
    sisters and the inexperienced sisters!
Far breath'd land! Arctic braced! Mexican breez'd! the
    diverse! the compact!

The Pennsylvanian! the Virginian! the double-
    Carolinian!
O all and each well-loved by me! my intrepid nations!
    O I at any rate include you all with perfect love!
I cannot be discharged from you! not from one any
    sooner than another!
O death! O for all that, I am yet of you unseen this
    hour with irrepressible love,
Walking New England, a friend, a traveler,
Splashing my bare feet in the edge of the summer
    ripples on Paumanok's sands,
Crossing the prairies, dwelling again in Chicago,
    dwelling in every town,
Observing shows, births, improvements, structures,
    arts,
Listening to orators and oratresses in public halls,
Of and through the States as during life, each man and
    woman my neighbor,
The Louisianian, the Georgian, as near to me, and I as
    near to him and her,
The Mississippian and Arkansian yet with me, and I
    yet with any of them,
Yet upon the plains west of the spinal river, yet in my
    house of adobie,
Yet returning eastward, yet in the Seaside State or in
    Maryland,

Yet Kanadian cheerily braving the winter, the snow
and ice welcome to me,
Yet a true son either of Maine or of the Granite State,
or the Narragansett Bay State, or the Empire
State,
Yet sailing to other shores to annex the same, yet
welcoming every new brother,
Hereby applying these leaves to the new ones from the
hour they unite with the old ones,
Coming among the new ones myself to be their
companion and equal, coming personally to you
now,
Enjoining you to acts, characters, spectacles, with me.

XV

With me with firm holding, yet haste, haste on.

For your life adhere to me,
(I may have to be persuaded many times before I
consent to give myself really to you, but what of
that?
Must not Nature be persuaded many times?)

No dainty dolce affettuoso I,
Bearded, sun-burnt, gray-neck'd, forbidding, I have
arrived,

To be wrestled with as I pass for the solid prizes of the
      universe,
For such I afford whoever can persevere to win them.

XVI

On my way a moment I pause,
Here for you! and here for America!
Still the present I raise aloft, still the future of the
      States I harbinge and glad and sublime,
And for the past I pronounce what the air holds of the
      red aborigines.
The red aborigines,
Leaving natural breaths, sounds of rain and winds,
      calls as of birds and animals in the woods,
      syllabled to us for names,
Okonee, Koosa, Ottawa, Monongahela, Sauk, Natchez,
      Chattahoochee, Kaqueta, Oronoco,
Wabash, Miami, Saginaw, Chippewa, Oshkosh,
      Walla-Walla,
Leaving such to the States they melt, they depart,
      charging the water and the land with names.

XVII

Expanding and swift, henceforth,
Elements, breeds, adjustments, turbulent, quick and
      audacious,

A world primal again, vistas of glory incessant and
     branching,
A new race dominating previous ones and grander far,
     with new contests,
New politics, new literatures and religions, new
     inventions and arts.

These, my voice announcing – I will sleep no more but
     arise,
You oceans that have been calm within me! how I feel
     you, fathomless, stirring, preparing
     unprecedented waves and storms.

XVIII

See, steamers steaming through my poems,
See, in my poem immigrants continually coming and
     landing,
See, in arriere, the wigwam, the trail, the hunter's hut,
     the flat-boat, the maize-leaf, the claim, the rude
     fence, and the backwoods village,
See, on the one side the Western Sea and on the other
     the Eastern Sea, how they advance and retreat
     upon my poems as upon their own shores,
See, pastures and forests in my poems – see, animals
     wild and tame – see, beyond the Kaw, countless
     herds of buffalo feeding on short curly grass,

See, in my poems, cities, solid, vast, inland, with paved
      streets, with iron and stone edifices, ceaseless
      vehicles, and commerce,
See, the many-cylinder'd steam printing-press – see,
      the electric telegraph stretching across the
      continent,
See, through Atlantica's depths pulses American
      Europe reaching, pulses of Europe duly return'd,
See, the strong and quick locomotive as it departs,
      panting, blowing the steam-whistle,
See, ploughmen ploughing farms – see, miners digging
      mines – see, the numberless factories,
See, mechanics busy at their benches with tools – see
      from among them superior judges, philosophs,
      Presidents, emerge, drest in working dresses,
See, lounging through the shops and fields of the
      States, me well-belov'd, close-held by day and
      night,
Hear the loud echoes of my songs there – read the
      hints come at last.

XIX

O camerado close! O you and me at last, and us two
      only.
O a word to clear one's path ahead endlessly!
O something ecstatic and undemonstrable! O music
      wild!

O now I triumph – and you shall also;
O hand in hand – O wholesome pleasure – O one more
    desirer and lover!
O to haste firm holding – to haste, haste on with me.

1856

SONG OF MYSELF

I

I celebrate myself, and sing myself,
And what I assume you shall assume,
For every atom belonging to me as good belongs to
    you.

I loafe and invite my soul,
I lean and loafe at my ease observing a spear of
    summer grass.
My tongue, every atom of my blood, form'd from this
    soil, this air,
Born here of parents born here from parents the same,
    and their parents the same,
I, now thirty-seven years old in perfect health begin,
Hoping to cease not till death.

Creeds and schools in abeyance,
Retiring back a while sufficed at what they are, but
    never forgotten,
I harbor for good or bad, I permit to speak at every
    hazard,
Nature without check with original energy.

II

Houses and rooms are full of perfumes, the shelves are
    crowded with perfumes,
I breathe the fragrance myself and know it and like it,
The distillation would intoxicate me also, but I shall
    not let it.

The atmosphere is not a perfume, it has no taste of the
    distillation, it is odorless,
It is for my mouth forever, I am in love with it,
I will go to the bank by the wood and become
    undisguised and naked,
I am mad for it to be in contact with me.
The smoke of my own breath,
Echoes, ripples, buzz'd whispers, love-root, silk-
    thread, crotch and vine,
My respiration and inspiration, the beating of my
    heart, the passing of blood and air through my
    lungs,
The sniff of green leaves and dry leaves, and of the
    shore and dark-color'd sea-rocks, and of hay in
    the barn,
The sound of the belch'd words of my voice loos'd to
    the eddies of the wind,
A few light kisses, a few embraces, a reaching around
    of arms,

The play of shine and shade on the trees as the supple
    boughs wag,
The delight alone or in the rush of the streets, or along
    the fields and hill-sides,
The feeling of health, the full-noon trill, the song of
    me rising from bed and meeting the sun.

Have you reckon'd a thousand acres much? have you
    reckon'd the earth much?
Have you practis'd so long to learn to read?
Have you felt so proud to get at the meaning of
    poems?

Stop this day and night with me and you shall possess
    the origin of all poems,
You shall possess the good of the earth and sun, (there
    are millions of suns left,)
You shall no longer take things at second or third
    hand, nor look through the eyes of the dead, nor
    feed on the spectres in books,
You shall not look through my eyes either, nor take
    things from me,
You shall listen to all sides and filter them from your
    self.

III

I have heard what the talkers were talking, the talk of
    the beginning and the end,
But I do not talk of the beginning or the end.

There was never any more inception than there is now,
Nor any more youth or age than there is now,
And will never be any more perfection than there is
    now,
Nor any more heaven or hell than there is now.

Urge and urge and urge,
Always the procreant urge of the world.

Out of the dimness opposite equals advance, always
    substance and increase, always sex,
Always a knit of identity, always distinction, always a
    breed of life.

To elaborate is no avail, learn'd and unlearn'd feel that
    it is so.

Sure as the most certain sure, plumb in the uprights,
    well entretied, braced in the beams,
Stout as a horse, affectionate, haughty, electrical,
I and this mystery here we stand.

Clear and sweet is my soul, and clear and sweet is all
    that is not my soul.

Lack one lacks both, and the unseen is proved by the
    seen,
Till that becomes unseen and receives proof in its turn.

Showing the best and dividing it from the worst age
    vexes age,
Knowing the perfect fitness and equanimity of things,
    while they discuss I am silent, and go bathe and
    admire myself.

Welcome is every organ and attribute of me, and of
    any man hearty and clean,
Not an inch nor a particle of an inch is vile, and none
    shall be less familiar than the rest.

I am satisfied – I see, dance, laugh, sing;
As the hugging and loving bed-fellow sleeps at my side
    through the night, and withdraws at the peep of
    the day with stealthy tread,
Leaving me baskets cover'd with white towels swelling
    the house with their plenty,
Shall I postpone my acceptation and realization and
    scream at my eyes,
That they turn from gazing after and down the road,

And forthwith cipher and show me to a cent,
Exactly the value of one and exactly the value of two,
    and which is ahead?

IV

Trippers and askers surround me,
People I meet, the effect upon me of my early life or the
    ward and city I live in, or the nation,
The latest dates, discoveries, inventions, societies,
    authors old and new,
My dinner, dress, associates, looks, compliments, dues,
The real or fancied indifference of some man or woman
    I love,
The sickness of one of my folks or of myself, or ill-
    doing or loss or lack of money, or depressions or
    exaltations,
Battles, the horrors of fratricidal war, the fever of
    doubtful news, the fitful events:
These come to me days and nights and go from me
    again,
But they are not the Me myself.

Apart from the pulling and hauling stands what I am,
Stands amused, complacent, compassionating, idle,
    unitary,
Looks down, is erect, or bends an arm on an impalpable
    certain rest,

Looking with side-curved head curious what will come
    next,
Both in and out of the game and watching and
    wondering at it.

Backward I see in my own days where I sweated
    through fog with linguists and contenders,
I have no mockings or arguments, I witness and wait.

V

I believe in you my soul, the other I am must not abase
    itself to you,
And you must not be abased to the other.
Loafe with me on the grass, loose the stop from your
    throat,
Not words, not music or rhyme I want, not custom or
    lecture, not even the best,
Only the lull I like, the hum of your valvèd voice.

I mind how once we lay such a transparent summer
    morning,
How you settled your head athwart my hips and gently
    turn'd over upon me,
And parted the shirt from my bosom-bone, and
    plunged your tongue to my bare-stript heart,
And reach'd till you felt my beard, and reach'd till you
    held my feet.

Swiftly arose and spread around me the peace and
knowledge that pass all the argument of the
earth,
And I know that the hand of God is the promise of my
own,
And I know that the spirit of God is the brother of my
own,
And that all the men ever born are also my brothers,
and the women my sisters and lovers,

And that a kelson of the creation is love,
And limitless are leaves stiff or drooping in the fields,
And brown ants in the little wells beneath them,
And mossy scabs of the worm fence, heap'd stones,
elder, mullein and poke-weed.

VI

A child said *What is the grass?* fetching it to me with full
hands;
How could I answer the child? I do not know what it is
any more than he.

I guess it must be the flag of my disposition, out of
hopeful green stuff woven.

Or I guess it is the handkerchief of the Lord,
A scented gift and remembrancer designedly dropt,
Bearing the owner's name someway in the corners,
    that we may see and remark, and say *Whose?*

Or I guess the grass is itself a child, the produced babe
    of the vegetation.

Or I guess it is a uniform hieroglyphic,
And it means, Sprouting alike in broad zones and
    narrow zones,
Growing among black folks as among white,
Kanuck, Tuckahoe, Congressman, Cuff, I give them the
    same, I receive them the same.

And now it seems to me the beautiful uncut hair of
    graves.

Tenderly will I use you curling grass,
It may be you transpire from the breasts of young men,
It may be if I had known them I would have loved
    them,
It may be you are from old people, or from offspring
    taken soon out of their mothers' laps,
And here you are the mothers' laps.

This grass is very dark to be from the white heads of
     old mothers,
Darker than the colorless beards of old men,
Dark to come from under the faint red roofs of mouths.

O I perceive after all so many uttering tongues,
And I perceive they do not come from the roofs of
     mouths for nothing.

I wish I could translate the hints about the dead young
     men and women,
And the hints about old men and mothers, and the
     offspring taken soon out of their laps.

What do you think has become of the young and old
     men?
And what do you think has become of the women and
     children?

They are alive and well somewhere,
The smallest sprout shows there is really no death,
And if ever there was it led forward life, and does not
     wait at the end to arrest it,
And ceas'd the moment life appear'd.

All goes onward and outward, nothing collapses,
And to die is different from what any one supposed,
     and luckier.

VII

Has any one supposed it lucky to be born?
I hasten to inform him or her it is just as lucky to die,
    and I know it.

I pass death with the dying and birth with the new-
    wash'd babe, and am not contain'd between my
    hat and boots,
And peruse manifold objects, no two alike and every
    one good,
The earth good and the stars good, and their adjuncts
    all good.

I am not an earth nor an adjunct of an earth,
I am the mate and companion of people, all just as
    immortal and fathomless as myself,
(They do not know how immortal, but I know.)

Every kind for itself and its own, for me mine male and
    female,
For me those that have been boys and that love
    women,
For me the man that is proud and feels how it stings to
    be slighted,
For me the sweet-heart and the old maid, for me
    mothers and the mothers of mothers,
For me lips that have smiled, eyes that have shed tears,
For me children and the begetters of children.

Undrape! you are not guilty to me, nor stale nor
     discarded,
I see through the broadcloth and gingham whether or
     no,
And am around, tenacious, acquisitive, tireless, and
     cannot be shaken away.

VIII

The little one sleeps in its cradle,
I lift the gauze and look a long time, and silently brush
     away flies with my hand.

The youngster and the red-faced girl turn aside up the
     busy hill,
I peeringly view them from the top.

The suicide sprawls on the bloody floor of the
     bedroom,
I witness the corpse with its dabbled hair, I note where
     the pistol has fallen.

The blab of the pave, tires of carts, sluff of boot-soles,
     talk of the promenaders,
The heavy omnibus, the driver with his interrogaating
     thumb, the clank of the shod horses on the granite
     floor,

The snow-sleighs, clinking, shouted jokes, pelts of
    snow-balls,
The hurrahs for popular favorites, the fury of rous'd
    mobs,
The flap of the curtain'd litter, a sick man inside borne
    to the hospital,
The meeting of enemies, the sudden oath, the blows
    and fall,
The excited crowd, the policeman with his star quickly
    working his passage to the centre of the crowd,
The impassive stones that receive and return so many
    echoes,
What groans of over-fed or half-starv'd who fall
    sunstruck or in fits,
What exclamations of women taken suddenly who
    hurry home and give birth to babes,
What living and buried speech is always vibrating
    here, what howls restrain'd by decorum,
Arrests of criminals, slights, adulterous offers made,
    acceptances, rejections with convex lips,
I mind them or the show or resonance of them – I come
    and I depart.

IX

The big doors of the country barn stand open and
ready,
The dried grass of the harvest-time loads the slow-
drawn wagon,
The clear light plays on the brown gray and green
intertinged,
The armfuls are pack'd to the sagging mow.

I am there, I help, I came stretch'd atop of the load,
I felt its soft jolts, one leg reclined on the other,
I jump from the cross-beams and seize the clover and
timothy,
And roll head over heels and tangle my hair full of
wisps.

X

Alone far in the wilds and mountains I hunt,
Wandering amazed at my own lightness and glee,
In the late afternoon choosing a safe spot to pass the
night,
Kindling a fire and broiling the fresh-kill'd game,
Falling asleep on the gather'd leaves with my dog and
gun by my side.

The Yankee clipper is under her sky-sails, she cuts the
sparkle and scud,

My eyes settle the land, I bend at her prow or shout
  joyously from the deck.

The boatmen and clam-diggers arose early and stopt
  for me,
I tuck'd my trowser-ends in my boots and went and
  had a good time;
You should have been with us that day round the
  chowder-kettle.

I saw the marriage of the trapper in the open air in the
  far west, the bride was a red girl,
Her father and his friends sat near cross-legged and
  dumbly smoking, they had moccasins to their feet
  and large thick blankets hanging from their
  shoulders,
On a bank lounged the trapper, he was drest mostly in
  skins, his luxuriant beard and curls protected his
  neck, he held his bride by the hand,
She had long eyelashes, her head was bare, her coarse
  straight locks descended upon her voluptuous
  limbs and reach'd to her feet.

The runaway slave came to my house and stopt
  outside,
I heard his motions crackling the twigs of the
  woodpile,

Through the swung half-door of the kitchen I saw him
    limpsy and weak,
And went where he sat on a log and led him in and
    assured him,
And brought water and fill'd a tub for his sweated body
    and bruis'd feet,
And gave him a room that enter'd from my own, and
    gave him some coarse clean clothes,
And remember perfectly well his revolving eyes and
    his awkwardness,
And remember putting plasters on the galls of his neck
    and ankles;
He staid with me a week before he was recuperated and
    pass'd north,
I had him sit next me at table, my fire-lock lean'd in the
    corner.

XI

Twenty-eight young men bathe by the shore,
Twenty-eight young men and all so friendly;
Twenty-eight years of womanly life and all so
    lonesome.

She owns the fine house by the rise of the bank,
She hides handsome and richly drest aft the blinds of
    the window.

Which of the young men does she like the best?
Ah the homeliest of them is beautiful to her.

Where are you off to, lady? for I see you,
You splash in the water there, yet stay stock still in
      your room.

Dancing and laughing along the beach came the
      twenty-ninth bather,
The rest did not see her, but she saw them and loved
      them.

The beards of the young men glisten'd with wet, it ran
      from their long hair,
Little streams pass'd all over their bodies.

As unseen hand also pass'd over their bodies,
It descended tremblingly from their temples and ribs.

The young men float on their backs, their white bellies
      bulge to the sun, they do not ask who seizes fast to
      them,
They do not know who puffs and declines with pendant
      and bending arch,
They do not think whom they souse with spray.

XII

The butcher-boy puts off his killing-clothes, or
    sharpens his knife at the stall in the market,
I loiter enjoying his repartee and his shuffle and
    break-down.

Blacksmiths with grimed and hairy chests environ the
    anvil,
Each has his main-sledge, they are all out, there is a
    great heat in the fire.

From the cinder-strew'd threshold I follow their
    movements,
The lithe sheer of their waists plays even with their
    massive arms,
Overhand the hammers swing, overhand so slow,
    overhand so sure,
They do not hasten, each man hits in his place.

XIII

The negro holds firmly the reins of his four horses, the
    block swags underneath on its tied-over chain,
The negro that drives the long dray of the stone-yard,
    steady and tall he stands pois'd on one leg on the
    string-piece,
His blue shirt exposes his ample neck and breast and
    loosens over his hip-band,

His glance is calm and commanding, he tosses the
    slouch of his hat away from his forehead,
The sun falls on his crispy hair and mustache, falls on
    the black of his polish'd and perfect limbs.

I behold the picturesque giant and love him, and I do
    not stop there,
I go with the team also.

In me the caresser of life wherever moving, backward
    as well as forward sluing,
To niches aside and junior bending, not a person or
    object missing,
Absorbing all to myself and for this song.

Oxen that rattle the yoke and chain or halt in the leafy
    shade, what is that you express in your eyes?
It seems to me more than all the print I have read in
    my life.

My tread scares the wood-drake and wood-duck on my
    distant and day-long ramble,
They rise together, they slowly circle around.

I believe in those wing'd purposes,
And acknowledge red, yellow, white, playing within
    me,
And consider green and violet and the tufted crown
    intentional,
And do not call the tortoise unworthy because she is
    not something else,
And the jay in the woods never studied the gamut, yet
    trills pretty well to me,
And the look of the bay mare shames silliness out of
    me.

XIV

The wild gander leads his flock through the cool night,
Ya-honk he says, and sounds it down to me like an
    invitation,
The pert may suppose it meaningless, but I listening
    close,
Find its purpose and place up there toward the wintry
    sky.

The sharp-hoof'd moose of the north, the cat on the
    house-sill, the chickadee, the prairie-dog,
The litter of the grunting sow as they tug at her teats,
The brood of the turkey-hen and she with her half-
    spread wings,
I see in them and myself the same old law.

The press of my foot to the earth springs a hundred
    affections,
They scorn the best I can do to relate them.

I am enamour'd of growing out-doors,
Of men that live among cattle or taste of the ocean or
    woods,
Of the builders and steerers of ships and the wielders
    of axes and mauls, and the drivers of horses,
I can eat and sleep with them week in and week out.

What is commonest, cheapest, nearest, easiest, is Me,
Me going in for my chances, spending for vast returns,
Adorning myself to bestow myself on the first that
    will take me,
Not asking the sky to come down to my good will,
Scattering it freely forever.

XV

The pure contralto sings in the organ loft,
The carpenter dresses his plank, the tongue of his
    foreplane whistles its wild ascending lisp,
The married and unmarried children ride home to
    their Thanksgiving dinner,
The pilot seizes the king-pin, he heaves down with a
    strong arm,

The mate stands braced in the whale-boat, lance and
    harpoon are ready,
The duck-shooter walks by silent and cautious
    stretches,
The deacons are ordain'd with cross'd hands at the
    altar,
The spinning-girl retreats and advances to the hum of
    the big wheel,
The farmer stops by the bars as he walks on a First-
    day loafe and looks at the oats and rye,
The lunatic is carried at last to the asylum a confirm'd
    case,
(He will never sleep any more as he did in the cot in his
    mother's bed-room;)
The jour printer with gray head and gaunt jaws works
    at his case,
He turns his quid of tobacco while his eyes blurr with
    the manuscript;
The malform'd limbs are tied to the surgeon's table,
What is removed drops horribly in a pail;
The quadroon girl is sold at the auction-stand, the
    drunkard nods by the bar-room stove,
The machinist rolls up his sleeves, the policeman
    travels his beat, the gate-keeper marks who pass,
The young fellow drives the express-wagon, (I love
    him, though I do not know him;)

The half-breed straps on his light boots to compete in
	the race,
The western turkey-shooting draws old and young,
	some lean on their rifles, some sit on logs,
Out from the crowd steps the marksman, takes his
	position, levels his piece;
The groups of newly-come immigrants cover the
	wharf or levee,
As the wooly-pates hoe in the sugar-field, the overseer
	views them from his saddle,
The bugle calls in the ball-room, the gentlemen run for
	their partners, the dancers bow to each other,
The youth lies awake in the cedar-roof'd garret and
	harks to the musical rain,
The Wolverine sets traps on the creek that helps fill
	the Huron,
The squaw wrapt in her yellow-hemm'd cloth is
	offering moccasins and bead-bags for sale,
The connoisseur peers along the exhibition-gallery
	with half-shut eyes bent sideways,
As the deck-hands make fast the steamboat the plank is
	thrown for the shore-going passengers,
The young sister holds out the skein while the elder
	sister winds it off in a ball, and stops now and
	then for the knots,
The one-year wife is recovering and happy having a
	week ago borne her first child,

The clean-hair'd Yankee girl works with her sewing-
    machine or in the factory or mill,
The paving-man leans on his two-handed rammer, the
    reporter's lead flies swiftly over the note-book,
    the sign-painter is lettering with blue and gold,
The canal boy trots on the tow-path, the book-keeper
    counts at his desk, the shoemaker waxes his
    thread,
The conductor beats time for the band and all the
    performers follow him,
The child is baptized, the convert is making his first
    professions,
The regatta is spread on the bay, the race is begun,
    (how the white sails sparkle!)
The drover watching his drove sings out to them that
    would stray,
The pedler sweats with his pack on his back, (the
    purchaser higgling about the odd cent;)
The bride unrumples her white dress, the minute-hand
    of the clock moves slowly,
The opium-eater reclines with rigid head and just-
    open'd lips,
The prostitute draggles her shawl, her bonnet bobs on
    her tipsy and pimpled neck,
The crowd laugh at her blackguard oaths, the men jeer
    and wink to each other,
(Miserable! I do not laugh at your oaths nor jeer you;)

The President holding a cabinet council is surrounded
    by the great Secretaries,
On the peazza walk three matrons stately and friendly
    with twinied arms,
The crew of the fish-smack pack repeated layers of
    halibut in the hold,
The Missourian crosses the plains toting his wares and
    his cattle,
As the fare-collector goes through the train he gives
    notice by the jingling of loose change,
The floor-men are laying the floor, the tinners are
    tinning the roof, the masons are calling for
    mortar,
In single file each shouldering his hod pass onward the
    laborers;
Seasons pursuing each other the indescribable crowd is
    gather'd, it is the fourth of Seventh-month, (what
    salutes of cannon and small arms!)
Seasons pursuing each other the plougher ploughs, the
    mower mows, and the winter-grain falls in the
    ground;
Off on the lakes the pike-fisher watches and waits by
    the hole in the frozen surface,
The stumps stand thick round the clearing, the
    squatter strikes deep with his axe,
Flatboatmen make fast towards dusk near the cotton-
    wood or pecan-trees,

Coon-seekers go through the regions of the Red river
    or through those drain'd by the Tennessee, or
    through those of the Arkansas,
Torches shine in the dark that hangs on the
    Chattahooche or Altamahaw,
Patriarchs sit at supper with sons and grandsons and
    great-grandsons around them,
In walls of adobie, in canvas tents, rest hunters and
    trappers after their day's sport,
The city sleeps and the country sleeps,
The living sleep for their time, the dead sleep for their
    time,
The old husband sleeps by his wife and the young
    husband sleeps by his wife;
And these tend inward to me, and I tend outward to
    them,
And such as it is to be of these more or less I am,
And of these one and all I weave the song of myself.

XVI

I am of old and young, of the foolish as much as the
    wise,
Regardless of others, ever regardful of others,
Maternal as well as paternal, a child as well as a man,
Stuff'd with the stuff that is coarse and stuff'd with the
    stuff that is fine,

One of the Nation of many nations, the smallest the
same and the largest the same,
A Southerner soon as a Northerner, a planter
nonchalant and hospitable down by the Oconee I
live,
A Yankee bound my own way ready for trade, my
joints the limberest joints on earth and the
sternest joints on earth,
A Kentuckian walking the vale of the Elkhorn in my
deer-skin leggings, a Louisianian or Georgian,
A boatman over lakes or bays or along coasts, a
Hoosier, Badger, Buckeye;
At home on Kanadian snow-slopes or up in the bush, or
with fishermen off Newfoundland,
At home in the fleet of ice-boats, sailing with the rest
and tacking,
At home on the hills of Vermont or in the woods of
Maine, or the Texan ranch,
Comrade of Californians, comrade of free North-
Westerners, (loving their big proportions,)
Comrade of raftsmen and coalmen, comrade of all who
shake hands and welcome to drink and meat,
A learner with the simplest, a teacher of the
thoughtfullest,
A novice beginning yet experient of myriads of
seasons,
Of every hue and caste am I, of every rank and religion,

A farmer, mechanic, artist, gentleman, sailor, quaker,
Prisoner, fancy-man, rowdy, lawyer, physician, priest.

I resist any thing better than my own diversity,
Breathe the air but leave plenty after me,
And am not stuck up, and am in my place.

(The moth and the fish-eggs are in their place,
The bright suns I see and the dark suns I cannot see
     are in their place,
The palpable is in its place and the impalpable is in its
     place.)

XVII

These are really the thoughts of all men in all ages and
     lands, they are not original with me,
If they are not yours as much as mine they are nothing,
     or next to nothing,
If they are not the riddle and the untying of the riddle
     they are nothing,
If they are not just as close as they are distant they are
     nothing.

This is the grass that grows wherever the land is and
     the water is,
This the common air that bathes the globe.

XVIII

With music strong I come, with my cornets and my
    drums,
I play not marches for accepted victors only, I play
    marches for conquer'd and slain persons.

Have you heard that it was good to gain the day?
I also say it is good to fall, battles are lost in the same
    spirit in which they are won.

I beat and pound for the dead,
I blow through my embouchures my loudest and
    gayest for them.

Vivas to those who have fail'd!
And to those whose war-vessels sank in the sea!
And to those themselves who sank in the sea!
And to the generals that lost engagements, and all
    overcome heroes!
And the numberless unknown heroes equal to the
    greatest heroes known!

XIX

This is the meal equally set, this the meat for natural
    hunger,
It is for the wicked just the same as the righteous, I
    make appointments with all,

I will not have a single person slighted or left away,
The kept-woman, sponger, thief, are hereby invited,
The heavy-lipp'd slave is invited, the venerealee is
     invited;
There shall be no difference between them and the rest.

This is the press of a bashful hand, this the float and
     odor of hair,
This the touch of my lips to yours, this the murmur of
     yearning,
This the far-off depth and height reflecting my own
     face,
This the thoughtful merge of myself, and the outlet
     again.

Do you guess I have some intricate purpose?
Well I have, for the Fourth-month showers have, and
     the mica on the side of a rock has.

Do you take it I would astonish?
Does the daylight astonish? does the early redstart
     twittering through the woods?
Do I astonish more than they?

This hour I tell things in confidence,
I might not tell everybody, but I will tell you.

XX

Who goes there? hankering, gross, mystical, nude;
How is it I extract strength from the beef I eat?

What is a man anyhow? what am I? what are you?

All I mark as my own you shall offset it with your own,
Else it were time lost listening to me.

I do not snivel that snivel the world over,
That months are vacuums and the ground but wallow
        and filth.

Whimpering and truckling fold with powders for
        invalids, conformity, goes to the fourth-remov'd,
I wear my hat as I please indoors or out.

Why should I pray? why should I venerate and be
        ceremonious?

Having pried through the strata, analyzed to a hair,
        counsel'd with doctors and calculated close,
I find no sweeter fat than sticks to my own bones.

In all people I see myself, none more and not one a
        barley-corn less,
And the good or bad I say of myself I say of them.

I know I am solid and sound,
To me the converging objects of the universe
       perpetually flow,
All are written to me, and I must get what the writing
       means.
I know I am deathless,
I know this orbit of mine cannot be swept by a
       carpenter's compass,
I know I shall not pass like a child's carlacue cut with a
       burnt stick at night.

I know I am august,
I do not trouble my spirit to vindicate itself or be
       understood,
I see that the elementary laws never apologize,
(I reckon I behave no prouder than the level I plant my
       house by, after all.)

I exist as I am, that is enough,
If no other in the world be aware I sit content,
And if each and all be aware I sit content.

One world is aware and by far the largest to me, and
       that is myself,
And whether I come to my own to-day or in ten
       thousand or ten million years,
I can cheerfully take it now, or with equal cheerfulness
       I can wait.

My foothold is tenon'd and mortis'd in granite,
I laugh at what you call dissolution,
And I know the amplitude of time.

XXI

I am the poet of the Body and I am the poet of the Soul,
The pleasures of heaven are with me and the pains of
    hell are with me,
The first I graft and increase upon myself, the latter I
    translate into a new tongue.

I am the poet of the woman the same as the man,
And I say it is as great to be a woman as to be a man,
And I say there is nothing greater than the mother of
    men.

I chant the chant of dilation or pride,
We have had ducking and deprecating about enough,
I show that size is only development.

Have you outstript the rest? are you the President?
It is a trifle, they will more than arrive there every one,
    and still pass on.

I am he that walks with the tender and growing night,
I call to the earth and sea half-held by the night.

Press close bare-bosom'd night – press close magnetic
    nourishing night!
Night of south winds – night of the large few stars!
Still nodding night – mad naked summer night.

Smile O voluptuous cool-breath'd earth!
Earth of the slumbering and liquid trees!
Earth of departed sunset – earth of the mountains
    misty-topt!
Earth of the vitreous pour of the full moon just tinged
    with blue!
Earth of shine and dark mottling the tide of the river!
Earth of the limpid gray of clouds brighter and clearer
    for my sake!
Far-swooping elbow'd earth – rich apple-blossom'd
    earth!
Smile, for your lover comes.

Prodigal, you have given me love – therefore I to you
    give love!
O unspeakable passionate love.

XXII

You sea! I resign myself to you also – I guess what you
    mean,
I behold from the beach your crooked inviting fingers,
I believe you refuse to go back without feeling of me,

We must have a turn together, I undress, hurry me out
    of sight of the land,
Cushion me soft, rock me in billowy drowse,
Dash me with amorous wet, I can repay you.

Sea of stretch'd ground-swells,
Sea breathing broad and convulsive breaths,
Sea of the brine of life and of unshovell'd yet always-
    ready graves,
Howler and scooper of storms, capricious and dainty
    sea,
I am integral with you, I too am of one phase and of all
    phases.

Partaker of influx and efflux I, extoller of hate and
    conciliation,
Extoller of amies and those that sleep in each others'
    arms.

I am he attesting sympathy,
(Shall I make my list of things in the house and skip
    the house that supports them?)

I am not the poet of goodness only, I do not decline to
    be the poet of wickedness also.

What blurt is this about virtue and about vice?
Evil propels me and reform of evil propels me, I stand
    indifferent,
My gait is no fault-finder's or rejecter's gait,
I moisten the roots of all that has grown.

Did you fear some scrofula out of the unflagging
    pregnancy?
Did you guess the celestial laws are yet to be work'd
    over and rectified?

I find one side a balance and the antipodal side a
    balance,
Soft doctrine as steady help as stable doctrine,
Thoughts and deeds of the present our rouse and early
    start.

This minute that comes to me over the past decillions,
There is no better than it and now.

What behaved well in the past or behaves well to-day
    is not such a wonder,
The wonder is always and always how there can be a
    mean man or an infidel.

XXIII

Endless unfolding of words of ages!
And mine a word of the modern, the word En-Masse.

A word of the faith that never balks,
Here or henceforward it is all the same to me, I accept
　　　Time absolutely.

It alone is without flaw, it alone rounds and completes
　　　all,
That mystic baffling wonder alone completes all.

I accept Reality and dare not question it,
Materialism first and last imbuing.

Hurrah for positive science! long live exact
　　　demonstration!
Fetch stonecrop mixt with cedar and branches of lilac,
This is the lexicographer, this the chemist, this made a
　　　grammar of the old cartouches,
These mariners put the ship through dangerous
　　　unknown seas,
This is the geologist, this works with the scalpel, and
　　　this is a mathematician.

Gentlemen, to you the first honors always!
Your facts are useful, and yet they are not my dwelling,
I but enter by them to an area of my dwelling.

Less the reminders of properties told my words,
And more the reminders they of life untold, and of
     freedom and extrication,
And make short account of neuters and geldings, and
     favor men and women fully equipt,
And beat the gong of revolt, and stop with fugitives
     and them that plot and conspire.

XXIV

Walt Whitman, a kosmos, of Manhattan the son,
Turbulent, fleshy, sensual, eating, drinking and
     breeding,
No sentimentalist, no stander above men and women
     or apart from them,
No more modest than immodest.

Unscrew the locks from the doors!
Unscrew the doors themselves from their jambs!

Whoever degrades another degrades me,
And whatever is done or said returns at last to me.

Through me the afflatus surging and surging, through
me the current and index.

I speak the pass-word primeval, I give the sign of
democracy,
By God! I will accept nothing which all cannot have
their counterpart of on the same terms.

Through me many long dumb voices,
Voices of the interminable generations of prisoners
and slaves,
Voices of the diseas'd and despairing and of thieves
and dwarfs,
Voices of cycles of preparation and accretion,
And of the threads that connect the stars, and of
wombs and of the father-stuff,
And of the rights of them the others are down upon,
Of the deform'd, trivial, flat, foolish, despised,
Fog in the air, beetles rolling balls of dung.

Through me forbidden voices,
Voices of sexes and lusts, voices veil'd and I remove the
veil,
Voices indecent by me clarified and transfigur'd.

I do not press my fingers across my mouth,
I keep as delicate around the bowels as around the head
and heart,
Copulation is no more rank to me than death is.

I believe in the flesh and the appetites,
Seeing, hearing, feeling, are miracles, and each part
and tag of me is a miracle.

Divine am I inside and out, and I make holy whatever I
touch or am touch'd from,
The scent of these arm-pits aroma finer than prayer,
This head more than churches, bibles, and all the
creeds.

If I worship one thing more than another it shall be the
spread of my own body, or any part of it,
Translucent mould of me it shall be you!
Shaded ledges and rests it shall be you!
Firm masculine colter it shall be you!
Whatever goes to the tilth of me it shall be you!
You my rich blood! your milky stream pale strippings
of my life!
Breast that presses against other breasts it shall be
you!
My brain it shall be your occult convolutions!

Root of wash'd sweet-flag! timorous pond-snipe! nest
    of guarded duplicate eggs! it shall be you!
Mix'd tussled hay of head, beard, brawn, it shall be
    you!
Trickling sap of maple, fibre of manly wheat, it shall be
    you!
Sun so generous it shall be you!
Vapors lighting and shading my face it shall be you!
You sweaty brooks and dews it shall be you!
Winds whose soft-tickling genitals rub against me it
    shall be you!
Broad muscular fields, branches of live oak, loving
    lounger in my winding paths, it shall be you!
Hands I have taken, face I have kiss'd, mortal I have
    ever touch'd, it shall be you.

I dote on myself, there is a lot of me and all so luscious,
Each moment and whatever happens thrills me with
    joy,
I cannot tell how my ankles bend, nor whence the
    cause of my faintest wish,
Nor the cause of the friendship I emit, nor the cause of
    the friendship I take again.

That I walk up my stoop, I pause to consider if it really be,
A morning-glory at my window satisfies me more than
    the metaphysics of books.

To behold the day-break!
The little light fades the immense and diaphanous
    shadows,
The air tastes good to my palate.

Hefts of the moving world at innocent gambols
    silently rising freshly exuding,
Scooting obliquely high and low.

Something I cannot see puts upward libidinous prongs,
Seas of bright juice suffuse heaven.

The earth by the sky staid with, the daily close of their
    junction,
The heav'd challenge from the east that moment over
    my head,
The mocking taunt, See then whether you shall be
    master!

XXV

Dazzling and tremendous how quick the sun-rise
    would kill me,
If I could not now and always send sun-rise out of me.

We also ascend dazzling and tremendous as the sun,
We found our own O my soul in the calm and cool of
    the daybreak.

My voice goes after what my eyes cannot reach,
With the twirl of my tongue I encompass worlds and
        volumes of worlds.

Speech is the twin of my vision, it is unequal to
        measure itself,
It provokes me forever, it says sarcastically,
Walt you contain enough, why don't you let it out then?

Come now I will not be tantalized, you conceive too
        much of articulation,
Do you not know O speech how the buds beneath you
        are folded?
Waiting in gloom, protected by frost,
The dirt receding before my prophetical screams,
I underlying causes to balance them at last,
My knowledge my live parts, it keeping tally with the
        meaning of all things,
Happiness, (which whoever hears me let him or her set
        out in search of this day.)

My final merit I refuse you, I refuse putting from me
        what I really am,
Encompass worlds, but never try to encompass me,
I crowd your sleekest and best by simply looking
        toward you.

Writing and talk do not prove me,
I carry the plenum of proof and every thing else in my
    face,
With the hush of my lips I wholly confound the
    skeptic.

XXVI

Now I will do nothing but listen,
To accrue what I hear into this song, to let sounds
    contribute toward it.

I hear bravuras of birds, bustle of growing wheat,
    gossip of flames, clack of sticks cooking my meals,
I hear the sound I love, the sound of the human voice,
I hear all sounds running together, combined, fused or
    following,
Sounds of the city and sounds out of the city, sounds of
    the day and night,
Talkative young ones to those that like them, the loud
    laugh of work-people at their meals,
The angry base of disjointed friendship, the faint tones
    of the sick,
The judge with hands tight to the desk, his pallid lips
    pronouncing a death-sentence,
The heave'e'yo of stevedores unlading ships by the
    wharves, the refrain of the anchor-lifters,
The ring of alarm-bells, the cry of fire, the whirr of

swift-streaking engines and hose-carts with
    premonitory tinkles and color'd lights,
The steam-whistle, the solid roll of the train of
    approaching cars,
The slow march play'd at the head of the association
    marching two and two,
(They go to guard some corpse, the flag-tops are
    draped with black muslin.)

I hear the violoncello, ('tis the young man's heart's
    complaint,)
I hear the key'd cornet, it glides quickly in through my
    ears,
It shakes mad-sweet pangs through my belly and
    breast.

I hear the chorus, it is a grand opera,
Ah this indeed is music – this suits me.

A tenor large and fresh as the creation fills me,
The orbic flex of his mouth is pouring and filling me
    full.

I hear the train'd soprano (what work with hers is
    this?)
The orchestra whirls me wider than Uranus flies,

It wrenches such ardors from me I did not know I
    possess'd them,
It sails me, I dab with bare feet, they are lick'd by the
    indolent waves,
I am cut by bitter and angry hail, I lose my breath,
Steep'd amid honey'd morphine, my windpipe throttled
    in fakes of death,
At length let up again to feel the puzzle of puzzles,
And that we call Being.

XXVII

To be in any form, what is that?
(Round and round we go, all of us, and ever come back
    thither,)
If nothing lay more develop'd the quahaug in its
    callous shell were enough.

Mine is no callous shell,
I have instant conductors all over me whether I pass or
    stop,
They seize every object and lead it harmlessly through
    me.

I merely stir, press, feel with my fingers, and am happy,
To touch my person to some one else's is about as
    much as I can stand.

XXVIII

Is this then a touch? quivering me to a new identity,
Flames and ether making a rush for my veins,
Treacherous tip of me reaching and crowding to help
    them,
My flesh and blood playing out lightning to strike
    what is hardly different from myself,
On all sides prurient provokers stiffening my limbs,
Straining the udder of my heart for its withheld drip,
Behaving licentious toward me, taking no denial,
Depriving me of my best as for a purpose,
Unbuttoning my clothes, holding me by the bare waist,
Deluding my confusion with the calm of the sunlight
    and pasture-fields,
Immodestly sliding the fellow-senses away,
They bribed to swap off with touch and go and graze at
    the edges of me,
No consideration, no regard for my draining strength
    or my anger,
Fetching the rest of the herd around to enjoy them a
    while,
Then all uniting to stand on a headland and worry me.

The sentries desert every other part of me,
They have left me helpless to a red marauder,
They all come to the headland to witness and assist
    against me.

I am given up by traitors,
I talk wildly, I have lost my wits, I and nobody else am
      the greatest traitor,
I went myself first to the headland, my own hands
      carried me there.

You villain touch! what are you doing? my breath is
      tight in its throat,
Unclench your floodgates, you are too much for me.

XXIX
Blind loving wrestling touch, sheath'd hooded sharp-
      tooth'd touch!
Did it make you ache so, leaving me?

Parting track'd by arriving, perpetual payment of
      perpetual loan,
Rich showering rain, and recompense richer afterward.

Sprouts take and accumulate, stand by the curb prolific
      and vital,
Landscapes projected masculine, full-sized and golden.

XXX
All truths wait in all things,
They neither hasten their own delivery nor resist it,
They do not need the obstetric forceps of the surgeon,

The insignificant is as big to me as any,
(What is less or more than a touch?)

Logic and sermons never convince,
The damp of the night drives deeper into my soul.

(Only what proves itself to every man and woman is
      so,
Only what nobody denies is so.)

A minute and a drop of me settle my brain,
I believe the soggy clods shall become lovers and
      lamps,
And a compend of compends is the meat of a man or
      woman,
And a summit and flower there is the feeling they have
      for each other,
And they are to branch boundlessly out of that lesson
      until it becomes omnific,
And until one and all shall delight us, and we them.

XXXI

I believe a leaf of grass is no less than the journey-
      work of the stars,
And the pismire is equally perfect, and a grain of sand,
      and the egg of the wren,
And the tree-toad is a chef-d'œuvre for the highest,

And the running blackberry would adorn the parlors
    of heaven,
And the narrowest hinge in my hand puts to scorn all
    machinery,
And the cow crunching with depress'd head surpasses
    any statue,
And a mouse is miracle enough to stagger sextillions
    of infidels.

I find I incorporate gneiss, coal, long-threaded moss,
    fruits, grains, esculent roots,
And am stucco'd with quadrupeds and birds all over,
And have distanced what is behind me for good
    reasons,
But call any thing back again when I desire it.

In vain the speeding or shyness,
In vain the plutonic rocks send their old heat against
    my approach,
In vain the mastodon retreats beneath its own
    powder'd bones,
In vain objects stand leagues off and assume manifold
    shapes,
In vain the ocean settling in hollows and the great
    monsters lying low,
In vain the buzzard houses herself with the sky,
In vain the snake slides through the creepers and logs,

In vain the elk takes to the inner passes of the woods,
In vain the razor-bill'd auk sails far north to Labrador,
I follow quickly, I ascend to the nest in the fissure of
    the cliff.

XXXII

I think I could turn and live with animals, they are so
    placid and self-contain'd,
I stand and look at them long and long.

They do not sweat and whine about their condition,
They do not lie awake in the dark and weep for their
    sins,
They do not make me sick discussing their duty to
    God,
Not one is dissatisfied, not one is demented with the
    mania of owning things,
Not one kneels to another, nor to his kind that lived
    thousands of years ago,
Not one is respectable or unhappy over the whole
    earth.

So they show their relations to me and I accept them,
They bring me tokens of myself, they evince them
    plainly in their possession.

I wonder where they get those tokens,
Did I pass that way huge times ago and negligently
    drop them?

Myself moving forward then and now and forever,
Gathering and showing more always and with
    velocity,
Infinite and omnigenous, and the like of these among
    them,
Not too exclusive toward the reachers of my
    remembrancers,
Picking out here one that I love, and now go with him
    on brotherly terms.

A gigantic beauty of a stallion, fresh and responsive to
    my caresses,
Head high in the forehead, wide between the ears,
Limbs glossy and supple, tail dusting the ground,
Eyes full of sparkling wickedness, ears finely cut,
    flexibly moving.

His nostrils dilate as my heels embrace him,
His well-built limbs tremble with pleasure as we race
    around and return.

I but use you a minute, then I resign you, stallion,
Why do I need your paces when I myself out-gallop
    them?
Even as I stand or sit passing faster than you.

XXXIII

Space and Time! now I see it is true, what I guess'd at,
What I guess'd when I loaf'd on the grass,
What I guess'd while I lay alone in my bed,
And again as I walk'd the beach under the paling stars
    of the morning.

My ties and ballasts leave me, my elbows rest in
    sea-gaps,
I skirt sierras, my palms cover continents,
I am afoot with my vision.

By the city's quadrangular houses – in log huts,
    camping with lumbermen,
Along the ruts of the turnpike, along the dry gulch and
    rivulet bed,
Weeding my onion-patch or hoeing rows of carrots
    and parsnips, crossing savannas, trailing in
    forests,
Prospecting, gold-digging, girdling the trees of a new
    purchase,

Scorch'd ankle-deep by the hot sand, hauling by boat
    down the shallow river,
Where the panther walks to and fro on a limb
    overhead, where the buck turns furiously at the
    hunter,
Where the rattlesnake suns his flabby length on a rock,
    where the otter is feeding on fish,
Where the alligator in his tough pimples sleeps by the
    bayou,
Where the black bear is searching for roots or honey,
    where the beaver pats the mud with his paddle-
    shaped tail;
Over the growing sugar, over the yellow-flower'd
    cotton plant, over the rice in its low moist field,
Over the sharp-peak'd farm house, with its scallop'd
    scum and slender shoots from the gutters,
Over the western persimmon, over the long-leav'd
    corn, over the delicate blue-flower flax,
Over the white and brown buckwheat, a hummer and
    buzzer there with the rest,
Over the dusky green of the rye as it ripples and
    shades in the breeze;
Scaling mountains, pulling myself cautiously up,
    holding on by low scragged limbs,
Walking the path worn in the grass and beat through
    the leaves of the brush,

Where the quail is whistling betwixt the woods and
the wheat-lot,
Where the bat flies in the Seventh-month eve, where
the great goldbug drops through the dark,
Where the brook puts out of the roots of the old tree
and flows to the meadow,
Where cattle stand and shake away flies with the
tremulous shuddering of their hides,
Where the cheese-cloth hangs in the kitchen, where
andirons straddle the hearth-slab, where cobwebs
fall in festoons from the rafters;
Where trip-hammers crash, where the press is
whirling its cylinders,
Wherever the human heart beats with terrible throes
under its ribs,
Where the pear-shaped balloon is floating aloft,
(floating in it myself and looking composedly
down,)
Where the life-car is drawn on the slip-noose, where
the heat hatches pale-green eggs in the dented
sand,
Where the she-whale swims with her calf and never
forsakes it,
Where the steam-ship trails hind-ways its long
pennant of smoke,
Where the fin of the shark cuts like a black chip out of
the water,

Where the half-burn'd brig is riding on unknown
      currents,
Where shells grow to her slimy deck, where the dead
      are corrupting below;
Where the dense-starr'd flag is borne at the head of the
      regiments,
Approaching Manhattan up by the long-stretching
      island,
Under Niagara, the cataract falling like a veil over my
      countenance,
Upon a door-step, upon the horse-block of hard wood
      outside,
Upon the race-course, or enjoying picnics or jigs or a
      good game of baseball,
At he-festivals, with blackguard gibes, ironical license,
      bull-dances, drinking, laughter,
At the cider-mill tasting the sweets of the brown mash,
      sucking the juice through a straw,
At apple-peelings wanting kisses for all the red fruit I
      find,
At musters, beach-parties, friendly bees, huskings,
      house-raisings;
Where the mocking-bird sounds his delicious gurgles,
      cackles, screams, weeps,
Where the hay-rick stands in the barn-yard, where the
      dry-stalks are scatter'd, where the brood-cow
      waits in the hovel,

Where the bull advances to do his masculine work,
     where the stud to the mare, where the cock is
     treading the hen,
Where the heifers browse, where geese nip their food
     with short jerks,
Where sun-down shadows lengthen over the limitless
     and lonesome prairie,
Where herds of buffalo make a crawling spread of the
     square miles far and near,
Where the humming-bird shimmers, where the neck of
     the long-lived swan is curving and winding,
Where the laughing-gull scoots by the shore, where
     she laughs her near-human laugh,
Where bee-hives range on a gray bench in the garden
     half hid by the high weeds,
Where band-neck'd partridges roost in a ring on the
     ground with their heads out,
Where burial coaches enter the arch'd gates of a
     cemetery,
Where winter wolves bark amid wastes of snow and
     icicled trees,
Where the yellow-crown'd heron comes to the edge of
     the marsh at night and feeds upon small crabs,
Where the splash of swimmers and divers cools the
     warm noon,
Where the katy-did works her chromatic reed on the
     walnut-tree over the well,

Through patches of citrons and cucumbers with silver-
wired leaves,

Through the salt-lick or orange glade, or under conical
firs,

Through the gymnasium, through the curtain'd
saloon, through the office or public hall;

Pleas'd with the native and pleas'd with the foreign,
pleas'd with the new and old,

Pleas'd with the homely woman as well as the
handsome,

Pleas'd with the quakeress as she puts off her bonnet
and talks melodiously,

Pleas'd with the tune of the choir of the whitewash'd
church,

Pleas'd with the earnest words of the sweating
Methodist preacher, impress'd seriously at the
camp-meeting;

Looking in at the shop windows of Broadway the
whole forenoon, flatting the flesh of my nose on
the thick plate glass,

Wandering the same afternoon with my face turn'd up
to the clouds, or down a lane or along the beach,

My right and left arms round the sides of two friends,
and I in the middle;

Coming home with the silent and dark-cheek'd bush-
boy, (behind me he rides at the drape of the day,)

Far from the settlements studying the print of animals'
     feet, or the moccasin print,
By the cot in the hospital reaching lemonade to a
     feverish patient,
Nigh the coffin'd corpse when all is still, examining
     with a candle;
Voyaging to every port to dicker and adventure,
Hurrying with the modern crowd as eager and fickle as
     any,
Hot toward one I hate, ready in my madness to knife
     him,
Solitary at midnight in my back yard, my thoughts
     gone from me a long while,
Walking the old hills of Judaea with the beautiful
     gentle God by my side,
Speeding through space, speeding through heaven and
     the stars,
Speeding amid the seven satellites and the broad ring,
     and the diameter of eighty thousand miles,
Speeding with tail'd meteors, throwing fire-balls like
     the rest,
Carrying the crescent child that carries its own full
     mother in its belly,
Storming, enjoying, planning, loving, cautioning,
Backing and filling, appearing and disappearing,
I tread day and night such roads.

I visit the orchards of spheres and look at the product,
And look at quintillions ripen'd and look at quintillions
    green.

I fly those flights of a fluid and swallowing soul,
My course runs below the soundings of plummets.

I help myself to material and immaterial,
No guard can shut me off, no law prevent me.

I anchor my ship for a little while only,
My messengers continually cruise away or bring their
    returns to me.

I go hunting polar furs and the seal, leaping chasms
    with a pike-pointed staff, clinging to topples of
    brittle and blue.

I ascend to the foretruck,
I take my place late at night in the crow's-nest,
We sail the arctic sea, it is plenty light enough,
Through the clear atmosphere I stretch around on the
    wonderful beauty,
The enormous masses of ice pass me and I pass them,
    the scenery is plain in all directions,
The white-topt mountains show in the distance, I fling
    out my fancies toward them,

We are approaching some great battle-field in which
      we are soon to be engaged,
We pass the colossal outposts of the encampment, we
      pass with still feet and caution,
Or we are entering by the suburbs some vast and
      ruin'd city,
The blocks and fallen architecture more than all the
      living cities of the globe.

I am a free companion, I bivouac by invading
      watchfires,
I turn the bridegroom out of bed and stay with the
      bride myself,
I tighten her all night to my thighs and lips.

My voice is the wife's voice, the screech by the rail of
      the stairs,
They fetch my man's body up dripping and drown'd.

I understand the large hearts of heroes,
The courage of present times and all times,
How the skipper saw the crowded and rudderless
      wreck of the steam-ship, and Death chasing it up
      and down the storm,
How he knuckled tight and gave not back an inch, and
      was faithful of days and faithful of nights,
And chalk'd in large letters on a board, *Be of good cheer,*
      we will not desert you;

How he follow'd with them and tack'd with them three
    days and would not give it up,
How he saved the drifting company at last,
How the lank loose-gown'd women look'd when
    boated from the side of their prepared graves,
How the silent old-faced infants and the lifted sick, and
    the sharp-lipp'd unshaved men;
All this I swallow, it tastes good, I like it well, it
    becomes mine,
I am the man, I suffer'd, I was there.

The disdain and calmness of martyrs,
The mother of old, condemn'd for a witch, burnt with
    dry wood, her children gazing on,
The hounded slave that flags in the race, leans by the
    fence, blowing, cover'd with sweat,
The twinges that sting like needles his legs and neck,
    the murderous buckshot and the bullets,
All these I feel or am.

I am the hounded slave, I wince at the bite of the dogs,
Hell and despair are upon me, crack and again crack
    the marksmen,
I clutch the rails of the fence, my gore dribs, thinn'd
    with the ooze of my skin,

I fall on the weeds and stones,
The riders spur their unwilling horses, haul close,
Taunt my dizzy ears and beat me violently over the
    head with whip-stocks.

Agonies are one of my changes of garments,
I do not ask the wounded person how he feels, I myself
    become the wounded person,
My hurts turn livid upon me as I lean on a cane and
    observe.

I am the mash'd fireman with breast-bone broken,
Tumbling walls buried me in their debris,
Heat and smoke I inspired, I heard the yelling shouts
    of my comrades,
I heard the distant click of their picks and shovels,
They have clear'd the beams away, they tenderly lift
    me forth.

I lie in the night air in my red shirt, the pervading hush
    is for my sake,
Painless after all I lie exhausted but not so unhappy,
White and beautiful are the faces around me, the heads
    are bared of their fire-caps,
The kneeling crowd fades with the light of the torches.

Distant and dead resuscitate,
They show as the dial or move as the hands of me, I am
     the clock myself.

I am an old artillerist, I tell of my fort's bombardment,
I am there again.

Again the long roll of the drummers,
Again the attacking cannon, mortars,
Again to my listening ears the cannon responsive.

I take part, I see and hear the whole,
The cries, curses, roar, the plaudits for well-aim'd
     shots,
The ambulanza slowly passing trailing its red drip,
Workingmen searching after damages, making
     indispensable repairs,
The fall of grenades through the rent roof, the fan-
     shaped explosion,
The whizz of limbs, heads, stone, wood, iron, high in
     the air.

Again gurgles the mouth of my dying general, he
     furiously waves with his hand,
He gasps through the clot *Mind not me – mind – the
     entrenchments.*

XXXIV

Now I tell what I knew in Texas in my early youth,
(I tell not the fall of Alamo,
Not one escaped to tell the fall of Alamo,
The hundred and fifty are dumb yet at Alamo,)
'Tis the tale of the murder in cold blood of four
      hundred and twelve young men.

Retreating they had form'd in a hollow square with
      their baggage for breastworks,
Nine hundred lives out of the surrounding enemy's,
      nine times their number, was the price they took
      in advance,
Their colonel was wounded and their ammunition
      gone,
They treated for an honorable capitulation, receiv'd
      writing and seal, gave up their arms and march'd
      back prisoners of war.

They were the glory of the race of rangers,
Matchless with horse, rifle, song, supper, courtship,
Large, turbulent, generous, handsome, proud, and
      affectionate,
Bearded, sunburnt, drest in the free costume of
      hunters,
Not a single one over thirty years of age.

The second First-day morning they were brought out
in squads and massacred, it was beautiful early
summer,
The work commenced about five o'clock and was over
by eight.

None obey'd the command to kneel,
Some made a mad and helpless rush, some stood stark
and straight,
A few fell at once, shot in the temple or heart, the
living and dead lay together,
The maim'd and mangled dug in the dirt, the new-
comers saw them there,
Some half-kill'd attempted to crawl away,
These were despatch'd with bayonets or batter'd with
the blunts of muskets,
A youth not seventeen years old seiz'd his assassin till
two more came to release him,
The three were all torn and cover'd with the boy's
blood.

At eleven o'clock began the burning of the bodies;
That is the tale of the murder of the four hundred and
twelve young men.

XXXV

Would you hear of an old-time sea-fight?
Would you learn who won by the light of the moon
    and stars?
List to the yarn, as my grandmother's father the sailor
    told it to me.

Our foe was no skulk in his ship I tell you, (said he,)
His was the surly English pluck, and there is no
    tougher or truer, and never was, and never will
    be;
Along the lower'd eve he came horribly raking us.

We closed with him, the yards entangled, the cannon
    touch'd,
My captain lash'd fast with his own hands.

We had receiv'd some eighteen pound shots under the
    water,
On our lower-gun-deck two large pieces had burst at
    the first fire, killing all around and blowing up
    overhead.

Fighting at sun-down, fighting at dark,
Ten o'clock at night, the full moon well up, our leaks
    on the gain, and five feet of water reported,

The master-at-arms loosing the prisoners confined in
the after-hold to give them a chance for
themselves.

The transit to and from the magazine is now stopt by
the sentinels,
They see so many strange faces they do not know
whom to trust.

Our frigate takes fire,
The other asks if we demand quarter?
If our colors are struck and the fighting done?

Now I laugh content, for I hear the voice of my little·
captain,
We have not struck, he composedly cries, *we have just
begun our part of the fighting.*

Only three guns are in use,
One is directed by the captain himself against the
enemy's mainmast,
Two well serv'd with grape and canister silence his
musketry and clear his decks.

The tops alone second the fire of this little battery,
especially the main-top,
They hold out bravely during the whole of the action.

Not a moment's cease,
The leaks gain fast on the pumps, the fire eats toward
    the powder-magazine.

One of the pumps has been shot away, it is generally
    thought we are sinking.

Serene stands the little captain,
He is not hurried, his voice is neither high nor low,
His eyes give more light to us than our battle-lanterns.

Toward twelve there in the beams of the moon they
    surrender to us.

XXXVI

Stretch'd and still lies the midnight,
Two great hulls motionless on the breast of the
    darkness,
Our vessel riddled and slowly sinking, preparations to
    pass to the one we have conquer'd,
The captain on the quarter-deck coldly giving his
    orders through a countenance white as a sheet,
Near by the corpse of the child that serv'd in the cabin,
The dead face of an old salt with long white hair and
    carefully curl'd whiskers,
The flames spite of all that can be done flickering aloft
    and below,

The husky voices of the two or three officers yet fit for
        duty,
Formless stacks of bodies and bodies by themselves,
        dabs of flesh upon the masts and spars,
Cut of cordage, dangle of rigging, slight shock of the
        soothe of waves,
Black and impassive guns, litter of powder-parcels,
        strong scent,
A few large stars overhead, silent and mournful
        shining,
Delicate sniffs of sea-breeze, smells of sedgy grass and
        fields by the shore, death-messages given in
        charge to survivors,
The hiss of the surgeon's knife, the gnawing teeth of
        his saw,
Wheeze, cluck, swash of falling blood, short wild
        scream, and long, dull, tapering groan,
These so, these irretrievable.

XXXVII

You laggards there on guard! look to your arms!
In at the conquer'd doors they crowd! I am possess'd!
Embody all presences outlaw'd or suffering,
See myself in prison shaped like another man,
And feel the dull unintermitted pain.

For me the keepers of convicts shoulder their carbines
    and keep watch,
It is I let out in the morning and barr'd at night.

Not a mutineer walks handcuff'd to jail but I am
    handcuff'd to him and walk by his side,
(I am less the jolly one there, and more the silent one
    with sweat on my twitching lips.)

Not a youngster is taken for larceny but I go up too,
    and am tried and sentenced.

Not a cholera patient lies at the last gasp but I also lie
    at the last gasp,
My face is ash-color'd, my sinews gnarl, away from me
    people retreat.

Askers embody themselves in me and I am embodied in
    them,
I project my hat, sit shame-faced, and beg.

XXXVIII

Enough! enough! enough!
Somehow I have been stunn'd. Stand back!
Give me a little time beyond my cuff'd head, slumbers,
    dreams, gaping,
I discover myself on the verge of a usual mistake.

That I could forget the mockers and insults!
That I could forget the trickling tears and the blows of
     the bludgeons and hammers!
That I could look with a separate look on my own
     crucifixion and bloody crowning.

I remember now,
I resume the overstaid fraction,
The grave of rock multiplies what has been confined to
     it, or to any graves,
Corpses rise, gashes heal, fastenings roll from me.

I troop forth replenish'd with supreme power, one of
     an average unending procession,
Inland and sea-coast we go, and pass all boundary
     lines,
Our swift ordinances on their way over the whole
     earth,
The blossoms we wear in our hats the growth of
     thousands of years.

Eleves, I salute you! come forward!
Continue your annotations, continue your
     questionings.

XXXIX

The friendly and flowing savage, who is he?
Is he waiting for civilization, or past it and mastering
    it?

Is he some Southwesterner rais'd out-doors? is he
    Kanadian?
Is he from the Mississippi country? Iowa, Oregon,
    California?
The mountains? prairie-life, bush-life? or sailor from
    the sea?

Wherever he goes men and women accept and desire
    him,
They desire he should like them, touch them, speak to
    them, stay with them.

Behavior lawless as snow-flakes, words simple as
    grass, uncomb'd head, laughter, and naiveté,
Slow-stepping feet, common features, common modes
    and emanations,
They descend in new forms from the tips of his fingers,
They are wafted with the odor of his body or breath,
    they fly out of the glance of his eyes.

XL

Flaunt of the sunshine I need not your bask – lie over!
You light surfaces only, I force surfaces and depths
    also.

Earth! you seem to look for something at my hands,
Say, old top-knot, what do you want?

Man or woman, I might tell how I like you, but cannot,
And might tell what it is in me and what it is in you,
    but cannot,
And might tell that pining I have, that pulse of my
    nights and days.

Behold, I do not give lectures or a little charity,
When I give I give myself.

You there, impotent, loose in the knees,
Open your scarf'd chops till I blow grit within you,
Spread your palms and lift the flaps of your pockets,
I am not to be denied, I compel, I have stores plenty
    and to spare,
And any thing I have I bestow.

I do not ask who you are, that is not important to me,
You can do nothing and be nothing but what I will
    infold you.

To cotton-field drudge or cleaner of privies I lean,
On his right cheek I put the family kiss,
And in my soul I swear I never will deny him.

On women fit for conception I start bigger and nimbler
    babes,
(This day I am jetting the stuff of far more arrogant
    republics.)

To any one dying, thither I speed and twist the knob of
    the door,
Turn the bed-clothes toward the foot of the bed,
Let the physician and the priest go home.

I seize the descending man and raise him with
    resistless will,
O despairer, here is my neck,
By God, you shall not go down! hang your whole
    weight upon me.

I dilate you with tremendous breath, I buoy you up,
Every room of the house do I fill with an arm'd force,
Lovers of me, bafflers of graves.

Sleep – I and they keep guard all night,
Not doubt, not decease shall dare to lay finger upon
    you,

I have embraced you, and henceforth possess you to
      myself,
And when you rise in the morning you will find what I
      tell you is so.

XLI

I am he bringing help for the sick as they pant on their
      backs,
And for strong upright men I bring yet more needed
      help.

I heard what was said of the universe,
Heard it and heard it of several thousand years;
It is middling well as far as it goes – but is that all?

Magnifying and applying come I,
Outbidding at the start the old cautious hucksters,
Taking myself the exact dimensions of Jehovah,
Lithographing Kronos, Zeus his son, and Hercules his
      grandson,
Buying drafts of Osiris, Isis, Belus, Brahma, Buddha,
In my portfolio placing Manito loose, Allah on a leaf,
      the crucifix engraved,
With Odin and the hideous-faced Mexitli and every
      idol and image,
Taking them all for what they are worth and not a cent
      more,

Admitting they were alive and did the work of their
days,
(They bore mites as for unfledg'd birds who have now
to rise and fly and sing for themselves,)
Accepting the rough deific sketches to fill out better in
myself, bestowing them freely on each man and
woman I see,
Discovering as much or more in a framer framing a
house,
Putting higher claims for him there with his roll'd-up
sleeves driving the mallet and chisel,
Not objecting to special revelations, considering a curl
of smoke or a hair on the back of my hand just as
curious as any revelation,
Lads ahold of fire-engines and hook-and-ladder ropes
no less to me than the gods of the antique wars,
Minding their voices peal through the crash of
destruction,
Their brawny limbs passing safe over charr'd laths,
their white foreheads whole and unhurt out of the
flames;
By the mechanic's wife with her babe at her nipple
interceding for every person born,
Three scythes at harvest whizzing in a row from three
lusty angels with shirts bagg'd out at their waists,
The snag-tooth'd hostler with red hair redeeming sins
past and to come,

Selling all he possesses, traveling on foot to fee lawyers
     for his brother and sit by him while he is tried for
     forgery;
What was strewn in the amplest strewing the square
     rod about me, and not filling the square rod then,
The bull and the bug never worshipp'd half enough,
Dung and dirt more admirable than was dream'd,
The supernatural of no account, myself waiting my
     time to be one of the supremes,
The day getting ready for me when I shall do as much
     good as the best, and be as prodigious;
By my life-lumps! becoming already a creator,
Putting myself here and now to the ambush'd womb of
     the shadows.

XLII

A call in the midst of the crowd,
My own voice, orotund sweeping and final.

Come my children,
Come my boys and girls, my women, household and
     intimates,
Now the performer launches his nerve, he has pass'd
     his prelude on the reeds within.

Easily written loose-finger'd chords – I feel the thrum
     of your climax and close.

My head slues round on my neck,
Music rolls, but not from the organ,
Folks are around me, but they are no household of
    mine.

Ever the hard unsunk ground,
Ever the eaters and drinkers, ever the upward and
    downward sun, ever the air and the ceaseless
    tides,
Ever myself and my neighbors, refreshing, wicked,
    real,
Ever the old inexplicable query, ever that thorn'd
    thumb, that breath of itches and thirsts,
Ever the vexer's *hoot! hoot!* till we find where the sly
    one hides and bring him forth,
Ever love, ever the sobbing liquid of life,
Ever the bandage under the chin, ever the trestles of
    death.

Here and there with dimes on the eyes walking,
To feed the greed of the belly the brains liberally
    spooning,
Tickets buying, taking, selling, but in to the feast
    never once going,
Many sweating, ploughing, thrashing, and then the
    chaff for payment receiving,
A few idly owning, and they the wheat continually
    claiming.

This is the city and I am one of the citizens,
Whatever interests the rest interests me, politics, wars,
    markets, newspapers, schools,
The mayor and councils, banks, tariffs, steamships,
    factories, stocks, stores, real estate and personal
    estate.

The little plentiful manikins skipping around in collars
    and tail'd coats,
I am aware who they are, (they are positively not
    worms or fleas,)
I acknowledge the duplicates of myself, the weakest
    and shallowest is deathless with me,
What I do and say the same waits for them,
Every thought that flounders in me the same flounders
    in them.

I know perfectly well my own egotism,
Know my omnivorous lines and must not write any
    less,
And would fetch you whoever you are flush with
    myself.

Not words of routine this song of mine,
But abruptly to question, to leap beyond yet nearer
    bring;
This printed and bound book – but the printer and the
    printing-office boy?

The well-taken photographs – but your wife or friend
      close and solid in your arms?
The black ship mail'd with iron, her mighty guns in her
      turrets – but the pluck of the captain and
      engineers?
In the houses the dishes and fare and furniture – but
      the host and hostess, and the look out of their
      eyes?
The sky up there – yet here or next door, or across the
      way?
The saints and sages in history – but you yourself?
Sermons, creeds, theology – but the fathomless human
      brain,
And what is reason? and what is love? and what is life?

XLIII

I do not despise you priests, all time, the world over,
My faith is the greatest of faiths and the least of faiths,
Enclosing worship ancient and modern and all
      between ancient and modern,
Believing I shall come again upon the earth after five
      thousand years,
Waiting responses from oracles, honoring the gods,
      saluting the sun,
Making a fetich of the first rock or stump, powowing
      with sticks in the circle of obis,
Helping the llama or brahmin as he trims the lamps of
      the idols,

Dancing yet through the streets in a phallic
      procession, rapt and austere in the woods a
      gymnosophist,
Drinking mead from the skull-cup, to Shastas and
      Vedas admirant, minding the Koran,
Walking the teokallis, spotted with gore from the
      stone and knife, beating the serpent-skin drum,
Accepting the Gospels, accepting him that was
      crucified, knowing assuredly that he is divine,
To the mass kneeling or the puritan's prayer rising, or
      sitting patiently in a pew,
Ranting and frothing in my insane crisis, or waiting
      dead-like till my spirit arouses me,
Looking forth on pavement and land, or outside of
      pavement and land,
Belonging to the winders of the circuit of circuits.

One of that centripetal and centrifugal gang I turn and
      talk like a man leaving charges before a journey.

Down-hearted doubters dull and excluded,
Frivolous, sullen, moping, angry, affected,
      dishearten'd, atheistical,
I know every one of you, I know the sea of torment,
      doubt, despair and unbelief.

How the flukes splash!
How they contort rapid as lightning, with spasms and
    spouts of blood!

Be at peace bloody flukes of doubters and sullen
    mopers,
I take my place among you as much as among any,
The past is the push of you, me, all, precisely the same,
And what is yet untried and afterward is for you, me,
    all, precisely the same.

I do not know what is untried and afterward,
But I know it will in its turn prove sufficient, and
    cannot fail.

Each who passes is consider'd, each who stops is
    consider'd, not a single one can it fail.

It cannot fail the young man who died and was buried,
Nor the young woman who died and was put by his
    side,
Nor the little child that peep'd in at the door, and then
    drew back and was never seen again,
Nor the old man who has lived without purpose, and
    feels it with bitterness worse than gall,
Nor him in the poor house tubercled by rum and the
    bad disorder,

Nor the numberless slaughter'd and wreck'd, nor the
    brutish koboo call'd the ordure of humanity,
Nor the sacs merely floating with open mouths for food
    to slip in,
Nor any thing in the earth, or down in the oldest
    graves of the earth,
Nor any thing in the myriads of spheres, nor the
    myriads of myriads that inhabit them,
Nor the present, nor the least wisp that is known.

XLIV

It is time to explain myself – let us stand up.

What is known I strip away,
I launch all men and women forward with me into the
    Unknown.

The clock indicates the moment – but what does
    eternity indicate?

We have thus far exhausted trillions of winters and
    summers,
There are trillions ahead, and trillions ahead of them.

Births have brought us richness and variety,
And other births will bring us richness and variety.

I do not call one greater and one smaller,
That which fills its period and place is equal to any.

Were mankind murderous or jealous upon you, my
    brother, my sister?
I am sorry for you, they are not murderous or jealous
    upon me,
All has been gentle with me, I keep no account with
    lamentation,
(What have I to do with lamentation?)

I am an acme of things accomplish'd, and I am encloser
    of things to be.

My feet strike an apex of the apices of the stairs,
On every step bunches of ages, and larger bunches
    between the steps,
All below duly travel'd, and still I mount and mount.

Rise after rise bow the phantoms behind me,
Afar down I see the huge first Nothing, I know I was
    even there,
I waited unseen and always, and slept through the
    lethargic mist,
And took my time, and took no hurt from the fetid
    carbon.

Long I was hugg'd close – long and long.

Immense have been the preparations for me,
Faithful and friendly the arms that have help'd me.

Cycles ferried my cradle, rowing and rowing like
    cheerful boatmen,
For room to me stars kept aside in their own rings,
They sent influences to look after what was to hold me.

Before I was born out of my mother generations
    guided me,
My embryo has never been torpid, nothing could
    overlay it.

For it the nebula cohered to an orb,
The long slow strata piled to rest it on,
Vast vegetables gave it sustenance,
Monstrous sauroids transported it in their mouths and
    deposited it with care.

All forces have been steadily employ'd to complete and
    delight me,
Now on this spot I stand with my robust soul.

XLV

O span of youth! ever-push'd elasticity!
O manhood, balanced, florid and full.

My lovers suffocate me,
Crowding my lips, thick in the pores of my skin,
Jostling me through streets and public halls, coming
    naked to me at night,
Crying by day *Ahoy!* from the rocks of the river,
    swinging and chirping over my head,
Calling my name from flower-beds, vines, tangled
    underbrush,
Lighting on every moment of my life,
Bussing my body with soft balsamic busses,
Noiselessly passing handfuls out of their hearts and
    giving them to be mine.

Old age superbly rising! O welcome, ineffable grace of
    dying days!

Every condition promulges not only itself, it
    promulges what grows after and out of itself,
And the dark hush promulges as much as any.

I open my scuttle at night and see the far-sprinkled
      systems,
And all I see multiplied as high as I can cipher edge but
      the rim of the farther systems.

Wider and wider they spread, expanding, always
      expanding,
Outward and outward and forever outward.

My sun has his sun and round him obediently wheels,
He joins with his partners a group of superior circuit,
And greater sets follow, making specks of the greatest
      inside them.

There is no stoppage and never can be stoppage,
If I, you, and the worlds, and all beneath or upon their
      surfaces, were this moment reduced back to a
      pallid float, it would not avail in the long run,
We should surely bring up again where we now stand,
And surely go as much farther, and then farther and
      farther.

A few quadrillions of eras, a few octillions of cubic
      leagues, do not hazard the span or make it
      impatient,
They are but parts, any thing is but a part.

See ever so far, there is limitless space outside of that,
Count ever so much, there is limitless time around
    that.

My rendezvous is appointed, it is certain,
The Lord will be there and wait till I come on perfect
    terms,
The great Camerado, the lover true for whom I pine
    will be there.

XLVI

I know I have the best of time and space, and was never
    measured and never will be measured.

I tramp a perpetual journey, (come listen all!)
My signs are a rain-proof coat, good shoes, and a staff
    cut from the woods,
No friend of mine takes his ease in my chair,
I have no chair, no church, no philosophy,
I lead no man to a dinner-table, library, exchange,
But each man and each woman of you I lead upon a
    knoll,
My left hand hooking you round the waist,
My right hand pointing to landscapes of continents
    and the public road.

Not I, not any one else can travel that road for you,
You must travel it for yourself.

It is not far, it is within reach,
Perhaps you have been on it since you were born and
did not know,
Perhaps it is everywhere on water and on land.

Shoulder your duds dear son, and I will mine, and let
us hasten forth,
Wonderful cities and free nations we shall fetch as we
go.

If you tire, give me both burdens, and the rest the chuff
of your hand on my hip,
And in due time you shall repay the same service to me,
For after we start we never lie by again.

This day before dawn I ascended a hill and look'd at the
crowded heaven,
And I said to my spirit *When we become the enfolders of
those orbs, and the pleasure and knowledge of every
thing in them, shall we be fill'd and satisfied then?*
And my spirit said *No, we but level that lift to pass and
continue beyond.*

You are also asking me questions and I hear you,
I answer that I cannot answer, you must find out for
      yourself.

Sit a while dear son,
Here are biscuits to eat and here is milk to drink,
But as soon as you sleep and renew yourself in sweet
      clothes, I kiss you with a good-by kiss and open
      the gate for your egress hence.

Long enough have you dream'd contemptible dreams,
Now I wash the gum from your eyes,
You must habit yourself to the dazzle of the light and
      of every moment of your life.

Long have you timidly waded holding a plank by the
      shore,
Now I will you to be a bold swimmer,
To jump off in the midst of the sea, rise again, nod to
      me, shout, and laughingly dash with your hair.

XLVII

I am the teacher of athletes,
He that by me spreads a wider breast than my own
      proves the width of my own,
He most honors my style who learns under it to
      destroy the teacher.

The boy I love, the same becomes a man not through
    derived power, but in his own right,
Wicked rather than virtuous out of conformity or fear,
Fond of his sweetheart, relishing well his steak,
Unrequited love or a slight cutting him worse than
    sharp steel cuts,
First-rate to ride, to fight, to hit the bull's eye, to sail a
    skiff, to sing a song or play on the banjo,
Preferring scars and the beard and faces pitted with
    small-pox over all latherers,
And those well-tann'd to those that keep out of the
    sun.

I teach straying from me, yet who can stray from me?
I follow you whoever you are from the present hour,
My words itch at your ears till you understand them.

I do not say these things for a dollar or to fill up the
    time while I wait for a boat,
(It is you talking just as much as myself, I act as the
    tongue of you,
Tied in your mouth, in mine it begins to be loosen'd.)

I swear I will never again mention love or death inside
    a house,
And I swear I will never translate myself at all, only to
    him or her who privately stays with me in the
    open air.

178

If you would understand me go to the heights or
    water-shore,
The nearest gnat is an explanation, and a drop or
    motion of waves a key,
The maul, the oar, the hand-saw, second my words.

No shutter'd room or school can commune with me,
But roughs and little children better than they.

The young mechanic is closest to me, he knows me
    well,
The woodman that takes his axe and jug with him shall
    take me with him all day,
The farm-boy ploughing in the field feels good at the
    sound of my voice,
In vessels that sail my words sail, I go with fishermen
    and seamen and love them.

The soldier camp'd or upon the march is mine,
On the night ere the pending battle many seek me, and
    I do not fail them,
On that solemn night (it may be their last) those that
    know me seek me.

My face rubs to the hunter's face when he lies down
    alone in his blanket,
The driver thinking of me does not mind the jolt of his
    wagon,

The young mother and old mother comprehend me,
The girl and the wife rest the needle a moment and
    forget where they are,
They and all would resume what I have told them.

XLVIII

I have said that the soul is not more than the body,
And I have said that the body is not more than the soul,
And nothing, not God, is greater to one than one's self
    is,
And whoever walks a furlong without sympathy walks
    to his own funeral drest in his shroud,
And I or you pocketless of a dime may purchase the
    pick of the earth,
And to glance with an eye or show a bean in its pod
    confounds the learning of all times,
And there is no trade or employment but the young
    man following it may become a hero,
And there is no object so soft but it makes a hub for the
    wheel'd universe,
And I say to any man or woman, Let your soul stand
    cool and composed before a million universes.

And I say to mankind, Be not curious about God,
For I who am curious about each am not curious about
    God,

(No array of terms can say how much I am at peace
     about God and about death.)

I hear and behold God in every object, yet understand
     God not in the least,
Nor do I understand who there can be more wonderful
     than myself.

Why should I wish to see God better than this day?
I see something of God each hour of the twenty-four,
     and each moment then,
In the faces of men and women I see God and in my
     own face in the glass,
I find letters from God dropt in the street, and every
     one is sign'd by God's name,
And I leave them where they are, for I know that
     wheresoe'er I go,
Others will punctually come for ever and ever.

XLIX

And as to you Death, and you bitter hug of mortality,
     it is idle to try to alarm me.

To his work without flinching the accoucheur comes,
I see the elder-hand pressing receiving supporting,
I recline by the sills of the exquisite flexible doors,
And mark the outlet, and mark the relief and escape.

And as to you Corpse I think you are good manure but
       that does not offend me,
I smell the white roses sweet-scented and growing,
I reach to the leafy lips, I reach to the polish'd breasts
       of melons.

And as to you Life I reckon you are the leavings of
       many deaths,
(No doubt I have died myself ten thousand times
       before.)

I hear you whispering there O stars of heaven,
O suns – O grass of graves – O perpetual transfers and
       promotions,
If you do not say any thing how can I say any thing?

Of the turbid pool that lies in the autumn forest,
Of the moon that descends the steeps of the soughing
       twilight,
Toss, sparkles of day and dusk – toss on the black
       stems that decay in the muck,
Toss to the moaning gibberish of the dry limbs.

I ascend from the moon, I ascend from the night,
I perceive that the ghastly glimmer is noonday
       sunbeams reflected,

And debouch to the steady and central from the
    offspring great or small.

L
There is that in me – I do not know what it is – but I
    know it is in me.

Wrench'd and sweaty – calm and cool then my body
    becomes,
I sleep – I sleep long.

I do not know it – it is without name – it is a word
    unsaid,
It is not in any dictionary, utterance, symbol.

Something it swings on more than the earth I swing
    on,
To it the creation is the friend whose embracing
    awakes me.

Perhaps I might tell more. Outlines! I plead for my
    brothers and sisters.

Do you see O my brothers and sisters?
It is not chaos or death – it is form, union, plan – it is
    eternal life – it is Happiness.

LI

The past and present wilt – I have fill'd them, emptied
    them
And proceed to fill my next fold of the future.

Listener up there! what have you to confide to me?
Look in my face while I snuff the sidle of evening,
(Talk honestly, no one else hears you, and I stay only a
    minute longer.)

Do I contradict myself?
Very well then I contradict myself,
(I am large, I contain multitudes.)

I concentrate toward them that are nigh, I wait on the
    door-slab.

Who has done his day's work? who will soonest be
    through with his supper?
Who wishes to walk with me?

Will you speak before I am gone? will you prove
    already too late?

LII

The spotted hawk swoops by and accuses me, he
    complains of my gab and my loitering.

I too am not a bit tamed, I too am untranslatable,
I sound my barbaric yawp over the roofs of the world.

The last scud of day holds back for me,
It flings my likeness after the rest and true as any on
    the shadow'd wilds,
It coaxes me to the vapor and the dusk.

I depart as air, I shake my white locks at the runaway
    sun,
I effuse my flesh eddies, and drift it in lacy jags.

I bequeath myself to the dirt to grow from the grass
    I love,
If you want me again look for me under your
    boot-soles.

You will hardly know who I am or what I mean,
But I shall be good health to you nevertheless,
And filter and fibre your blood.

Failing to fetch me at first keep encouraged,
Missing me one place search another,
I stop somewhere waiting for you.

1855

THE SLEEPERS

I

I wander all night in my vision,
Stepping with light feet .... swiftly and noiselessly
    stepping and stopping,
Bending with open eyes over the shut eyes of sleepers;
Wandering and confused .... lost to myself .... ill-
    assorted .... contradictory,
Pausing and gazing and bending and stopping.

How solemn they look there, stretched and still;
How quiet they breathe, the little children in their
    cradles.

The wretched features of ennuyees, the white features
    of corpses, the livid faces of drunkards, the sick-
    gray faces of onanists,
The gashed bodies on battlefields, the insane in their
    strong-doored rooms, the sacred idiots,
The newborn emerging from gates and the dying
    emerging from gates,
The night pervades them and enfolds them.

The married couple sleep calmly in their bed, he with
    his palm on the hip of the wife, and she with her
    palm on the hip of the husband,

The sisters sleep lovingly side by side in their bed,
The men sleep lovingly side by side in theirs,
And the mother sleeps with her little child carefully
     wrapped.

The blind sleep, and the deaf and dumb sleep,
The prisoner sleeps well in the prison .... the runaway
     son sleeps,
The murderer that is to be hung next day .... how does
     he sleep?
And the murdered person .... how does he sleep?

The female that loves unrequited sleeps,
And the male that loves unrequited sleeps;
The head of the moneymaker that plotted all day
     sleeps,
And the enraged and treacherous dispositions sleep.

I stand with drooping eyes by the worstsuffering and
     restless,
I pass my hands soothingly to and fro a few inches
     from them;
The restless sink in their beds .... they fitfully sleep.

The earth recedes from me into the night,
I saw that it was beautiful .... and I see that what is not
     the earth is beautiful.

I go from bedside to bedside .... I sleep close with the
   other sleepers, each in turn;
I dream in my dream all the dreams of the other
   dreamers,
And I become the other dreamers.

I am a dance .... Play up there! the fit is whirling me
   fast.

I am the everlaughing .... it is new moon and twilight,
I see the hiding of douceurs .... I see nimble ghosts
   whichever way I look,
Cache and cache again deep in the ground and sea, and
   where it is neither ground or sea.

Well do they do their jobs those journeymen divine,
Only from me can they hide nothing and would not if
   they could;
I reckon I am their boss, and they make me a pet
   besides,
And surround me, and lead me and run ahead when I
   walk,
And lift their cunning covers and signify me with
   stretched arms, and resume the way;
Onward we move, a gay gang of blackguards with
   mirthshouting music and wildflapping pennants
   of joy.

I am the actor and the actress .... the voter .. the
    politician,
The emigrant and the exile .. the criminal that stood in
    the box,
He who has been famous, and he who shall be famous
    after today,
The stammerer .... the wellformed person .. the
    wasted or feeble person.

I am she who adorned herself and folded her hair
    expectantly,
My truant lover has come and it is dark.

Double yourself and receive me darkness,
Receive me and my lover too .... he will not let me go
    without him.

I roll myself upon you as upon a bed .... I resign
    myself to the dusk.

He whom I call answers me and takes the place of my
    lover,
He rises with me silently from the bed.

Darkness you are gentler than my lover .... his flesh
    was sweaty and panting,
I feel the hot moisture yet that he left me.

My hands are spread forth .. I pass them in all
     directions,
I would sound up the shadowy shore to which you are
     journeying.

Be careful, darkness .... already, what was it touched
     me?
I thought my lover had gone .... else darkness and he
     are one,
I hear the heart-beat .... I follow .. I fade away.

O hotcheeked and blushing! O foolish hectic!
O for pity's sake, no one must see me now! .... my
     clothes were stolen while I was abed,
Now I am thrust forth, where shall I run?

Pier that I saw dimly last night when I looked from the
     windows,
Pier out from the main, let me catch myself with you
     and stay .... I will not chafe you;
I feel ashamed to go naked about the world,
And am curious to know where my feet stand .... and
     what is this flooding me, childhood or manhood
     .... and the hunger that crosses the bridge
     between.

The cloth laps a first sweet eating and drinking,
Laps life-swelling yolks .... laps ear of rose-corn,
     milky and just ripened;
The white teeth stay, and the boss-tooth advances in
     darkness,
And liquor is spilled on lips and bosoms by touching
     glasses, and the best liquor afterward.

II

I descend my western course .... my sinews are flaccid,
Perfume and youth course through me, and I am their
     wake.

It is my face yellow and wrinkled instead of the old
     woman's,
I sit low in a strawbottom chair and carefully darn my
     grandson's stockings.

It is I too .... the sleepless widow looking out on the
     winter midnight
I see the sparkles of starshine on the icy and pallid
     earth.

A shroud I see – and I am the shroud .... I wrap a body
     and lie in the coffin;
It is dark here underground .... it is not evil or pain
     here .... it is blank here, for reasons.

It seems to me that everything in the light and air
    ought to be happy;
Whoever is not in his coffin and the dark grave, let him
    know he has enough.

III

I see a beautiful gigantic swimmer swimming naked
    through the eddies of the sea,
His brown hair lies close and even to his head .... he
    strikes out with courageous arms .... he urges
    himself with his legs.

I see his white body .... I see his undaunted eyes;
I hate the swift-running eddies that would dash him
    headforemost on the rocks.

What are you doing you ruffianly red-trickled waves?
Will you kill the courageous giant? Will you kill him
    in the prime of his middle age?

Steady and long he struggles;
He is baffled and banged and bruised .... he holds out
    while his strength holds out,
The slapping eddies are spotted with his blood ....
    they bear him away .... they roll him and swing
    him and turn him:

His beautiful body is borne in the circling eddies .... it
is continually bruised on rocks,
Swiftly and out of sight is born the brave corpse.

IV

I turn but do not extricate myself;
Confused .... a pastreading .... another, but with
darkness yet.

The beach is cut by the razory ice-wind .... the wreck-
guns sound,
The tempest lulls and the moon comes floundering
through the drifts.

I look where the ship helplessly heads end on I
hear the burst as she strikes .... I hear the howls
of dismay .... they grow fainter and fainter.

I cannot aid with my wringing fingers;
I can but rush to the surf and let it drench me and
freeze upon me.

I search with the crowd .... not one of the company is
washed to us alive;
In the morning I help pick up the dead and lay them in
rows in a barn.

V

Now of the old war-days .. the defeat at Brooklyn;
Washington stands inside the lines .. he stands on the
 entrenched hills amid a crowd of officers,
His face is cold and damp .... he cannot repress the
 weeping drops .... he lifts the glass perpetually to
 his eyes .... the color is blanched from his cheeks,
He sees the slaughter of the southern braves confided
 to him by their parents.

The same at last and at last when peace is declared,
He stands in the room of the old tavern .... the
 wellbeloved soldiers all pass through.

The officers speechless and slow draw near in their
 turns,
The chief encircles their necks with his arm and kisses
 them on the cheek,
He kisses lightly the wet cheeks one after another ....
 he shakes hands and bids goodbye to the army.

VI

Now I tell what my mother told me today as we sat at
 dinner together,
Of when she was a nearly grown girl living home with
 her parents on the old homestead.

A red squaw came one breakfastime to the old
    homestead,
On her back she carried a bundle of rushes for
    rushbottoming chairs;
Her hair straight shiny coarse black and profuse
    halfenveloped her face,
Her step was free and elastic . . . . her voice sounded
    exquisitely as she spoke.

My mother looked in delight and amazement at the
    stranger,
She looked at the beauty of her tallborne face and full
    and pliant limbs,
The more she looked upon her she loved her,
Never before had she seen such wonderful beauty and
    purity;
She made her sit on a bench by the jamb of the fireplace . . .
    she cooked food for her,
She had no work to give her but she gave her
    remembrance and fondness.

The red squaw staid all the forenoon, and toward the
    middle of the afternoon she went away;
O my mother was loth to have her go away,
All the week she thought of her .... she watched for
    her many a month,
She remembered her many a winter and many a
    summer,
But the red squaw never came nor was heard of there
    again.

Now Lucifer was not dead .... or if he was I am his
    sorrowful terrible heir;
I have been wronged .... I am oppressed .... I hate him
    that oppresses me,
I will either destroy him, or he shall release me.

Damn him! how he does defile me,
How he informs against my brother and sister and
    takes pay for their blood,
How he laughs when I look down the bend after the
    steamboat that carries away my woman.

Now the vast dusk bulk that is the whale's bulk .... it
    seems mine,
Warily, sportsman! though I lie so sleepy and sluggish,
    my tap is death.

VII

A show of the summer softness .... a contact of
      something unseen .... an amour of the light and
      air;
I am jealous and overwhelmed with friendliness,
And will go gallivant with the light and the air myself,
And have an unseen something to be in contact with
      them also.

O love and summer! you are in the dreams and in me,
Autumn and winter are in the dreams .... the farmer
      goes with his thrift,
The droves and crops increase .... the barns are
      wellfilled.

Elements merge in the night .... ships make tacks in
      the dreams .... the sailor sails .... the exile
      returns home,
The fugitive returns unharmed .... the immigrant is
      back beyond months and years;
The poor Irishman lives in the simple house of his
      childhood, with the wellknown neighbors and
      faces,
They warmly welcome him .... he is barefoot again ....
      he forgets he is welloff;

The Dutchman voyages home, and the Scotchman and
     Welchman voyage home .. and the native of the
     Mediterranean voyages home;
To every port of England and France and Spain enter
     wellfilled ships;
The Swiss foots it toward his hills .... the Prussian
     goes his way, and the Hungarian his way, and the
     Pole goes his way,
The Swede returns, and the Dane and Norwegian
     return.

The homeward bound and the outward bound,
The beautiful lost swimmer, the ennuyee, the onanist,
     the female that loves unrequited, the
     moneymaker,
The actor and actress .. those through with their parts
     and those waiting to commence,
The affectionate boy, the husband and wife, the voter,
     the nominee that is chosen and the nominee that
     has failed,
The great already known, and the great anytime after
     to day,
The stammerer, the sick, the perfectformed, the
     homely,
The criminal that stood in the box, the judge that sat
     and sentenced him, the fluent lawyers, the jury,
     the audience,

The laugher and weeper, the dancer, the midnight
    widow, the red squaw,
The consumptive, the erysipalite, the idiot, he that is
    wronged,
The antipodes, and every one between this and them in
    the dark,
I swear they are averaged now .... one is no better
    than the other,
The night and sleep have likened them and restored
    them.

I swear they are all beautiful,
Every one that sleeps is beautiful .... every thing in the
    dim night is beautiful,
The wildest and bloodiest is over and all is peace.

Peace is always beautiful,
The myth of heaven indicates peace and night.

The myth of heaven indicates the soul;
The soul is always beautiful .... it appears more or it
    appears less .... it comes or lags behind,
It comes from its embowered garden and looks
    pleasantly on itself and encloses the world;
Perfect and clean the genitals previously jetting, and
    perfect and clean the womb cohering,

The head wellgrown and proportioned and plumb, and
the bowels and joints proportioned and plumb.

The soul is always beautiful,
The universe is duly in order .... every thing is in its
place,
What is arrived is in its place, and what waits is in its
place;
The twisted skull waits .... the watery or rotten blood
waits,
The child of the glutton or venerealee waits long, and
the child of the drunkard waits long, and the
drunkard himself waits long,
The sleepers that lived and died wait .... the far
advanced are to go on in their turns, and the far
behind are to go on in their turns,
The diverse shall be no less diverse, but they shall flow
and unite .... they unite now.

VIII

The sleepers are very beautiful as they lie unclothed,
They flow hand in hand over the whole earth from east
to west as they lie unclothed;
The Asiatic and African are hand in hand .. the
European and American are hand in hand,
Learned and unlearned are hand in hand .. and male
and female are hand in hand;

The bare arm of the girl crosses the bare breast of her
       lover .... they press close without lust .... his lips
       press her neck,
The father holds his grown or ungrown son in his
       arms with measureless love .... and the son holds
       the father in his arms with measureless love,
The white hair of the mother shines on the white wrist
       of the daughter,
The breath of the boy goes with the breath of the man
       .... friend is inarmed by friend,
The scholar kisses the teacher and the teacher kisses
       the scholar .... the wronged is made right,
The call of the slave is one with the master's call .. and
       the master salutes the slave,
The felon steps forth from the prison .... the insane
       becomes sane .... the suffering of sick persons is
       relieved,
The sweatings and fevers stop .. the throat that was
       unsound is sound .. the lungs of the consumptive
       are resumed .. the poor distressed head is free,
The joints of the rheumatic move as smoothly as ever,
       and smoother than ever,
Stiflings and passages open .... the paralysed become
       supple,
The swelled and convulsed and congested awake to
       themselves in condition,

They pass the invigoration of the night and the
chemistry of the night and awake.

I too pass from the night;
I stay awhile away O night, but I return to you again
and love you;
Why should I be afraid to trust myself to you?

I am not afraid .... I have been well brought forward
by you;
I love the rich running day, but I do not desert her in
whom I lay so long:
I know not how I came of you, and I know not where I
go with you .... but I know I came well and shall
go well.

I will stop only a time with the night .... and rise
betimes.

I will duly pass the day O my mother and duly return
to you;
Not you will yield forth the dawn again more surely
than you will yield forth me again,
Not the womb yield the babe in its time more surely
than I shall be yielded from you in my time.

1855

PASSAGE TO INDIA

I

Singing my days,
Singing the great achievements of the present,
Singing the strong light works of engineers,
Our modern wonders, (the antique ponderous Seven
      outvied,)
In the Old World the east the Suez canal,
The New by its mighty railroad spann'd,
The seas inlaid with eloquent gentle wires;
Yet first to sound, and ever sound, the cry with thee
      O soul,
The Past! the Past! the Past!

The Past – the dark unfathom'd retrospect!
The teeming gulf – the sleepers and the shadows!
The past – the infinite greatness of the past!
For what is the present after all but a growth out of the
      past?
(As a projectile form'd, impell'd, passing a certain line,
      still keeps on,
So the present, utterly form'd, impell'd by the past.)

II

Passage O soul to India!
Eclaircise the myths Asiatic, the primitive fables.
Not you alone proud truths of the world,
Nor you alone ye facts of modern science,
But myths and fables of eld, Asia's, Africa's fables,
The far-darting beams of the spirit, the unloos'd
      dreams,
The deep diving bibles and legends,
The daring plots of the poets, the elder religions;
O you temples fairer than lilies pour'd over by the
      rising sun!
O you fables spurning the known, eluding the hold of
      the known, mounting to heaven!
You lofty and dazzling towers, pinnacled, red as roses,
      burnish'd with gold!
Towers of fables immortal fashion'd from mortal
      dreams!
You too I welcome and fully the same as the rest!
You too with joy I sing.

Passage to India!
Lo, soul, seest thou not God's purpose from the first?
The earth to be spann'd, connected by network,
The races, neighbors, to marry and be given in
      marriage,

The oceans to be cross'd, the distant brought near,
The lands to be welded together.

A worship new I sing,
You captains, voyagers, explorers, yours,
You engineers, you architects, machinists, yours,
You, not for trade or transportation only,
But in God's name, and for thy sake O soul.

III

Passage to India!
Lo soul for thee of tableaus twain,
I see in one the Suez canal initiated, open'd,
I see the procession of steamships, the Empress
      Eugenie's leading the van,
I mark from on deck the strange landscape, the pure
      sky, the level sand in the distance,
I pass swifly the picturesque groups, the workmen
      gather'd,
The gigantic dredging machines.

In one again, different, (yet thine, all thine, O soul, the
      same,)
I see over my own continent the Pacific railroad
      surmounting every barrier,
I see continual trains of cars winding along the Platte
      carrying freight and passengers,

I hear the locomotives rushing and roaring, and the
    shrill steam-whistle,
I hear the echoes reverberate through the grandest
    scenery in the world,
I cross the Laramie plains, I note the rocks in
    grotesque shapes, the buttes,
I see the plentiful larkspur and wild onions, the barren,
    colorless, sage-deserts,
I see in glimpses afar or towering immediately above
    me the great mountains, I see the Wind river and
    the Wahsatch mountains,
I see the Monument mountain and the Eagle's Nest, I
    pass the Promontory, I ascend the Nevadas,
I scan the noble Elk mountain and wind around its
    base,
I see the Humboldt range, I thread the valley and cross
    the river,
I see the clear waters of lake Tahoe, I see forests of
    majestic pines,
Or crossing the great desert, the alkaline plains, I
    behold enchanting mirages of waters and
    meadows,
Marking through these and after all, in duplicate
    slender lines,
Bridging the three or four thousand miles of land
    travel,

Tying the Eastern to the Western sea,
The road between Europe and Asia.

(Ah Genoese thy dream! thy dream!
Centuries after thou art laid in thy grave,
The shore thou foundest verifies thy dream.)

IV

Passage to India!
Struggles of many a captain, tales of many a sailor
    dead,
Over my mood stealing and spreading they come,
Like clouds and cloudlets in the unreach'd sky.
Along all history, down the slopes,
As a rivulet running, sinking now, and now again to
    the surface rising,
A ceaseless thought, a varied train – lo, soul, to thee,
    thy sight, they rise,
The plans, the voyages again, the expeditions;
Again Vasco de Gama sails forth,
Again the knowledge gain'd, the mariner's compass,
Lands found and nations born, thou born America,
For purpose vast, man's long probation fill'd,
Thou rondure of the world at last accomplish'd.

V

O vast Rondure, swimming in space,
Cover'd all over with visible power and beauty,
Alternate light and day and the teeming spiritual
    darkness,
Unspeakable high processions of sun and moon and
    countless stars above,
Below, the manifold grass and waters, animals,
    mountains, trees,
With inscrutable purpose, some hidden prophetic
    intention,
Now first it seems my thought begins to span thee.

Down from the gardens of Asia descending radiating,
Adam and Eve appear, then their myriad progeny after
    them,
Wandering, yearning, curious, with restless
    explorations,
With questionings, baffled, formless, feverish, with
    never-happy hearts,
With that sad incessant refrain, *Wherefore unsatisfied*
    soul? and *Whither O mocking life?*

Ah who shall soothe these feverish children?
Who justify these restless explorations?
Who speak the secret of impassive earth?

Who bind it to us? what is this separate Nature so
    unnatural?
What is this earth to our affections? (unloving earth,
    without a throb to answer ours,
Cold earth, the place of graves.)

Yet soul be sure the first intent remains, and shall be
    carried out,
Perhaps even now the time has arrived.

After the seas are all cross'd, (as they seem already
    cross'd,)
After the great captains and engineers have
    accomplish'd their work,
After the noble inventors, after the scientists, the
    chemist, the geologist, ethnologist,
Finally shall come the poet worthy that name,
The true son of God shall come singing his songs.

Then not your deeds only O voyagers, O scientist and
    inventors, shall be justified,
All these hearts as of fretted children shall be sooth'd,
All affection shall be fully responded to, the secret shall
    be told,
All these separations and gaps shall be taken up and
    hook'd and link'd together,

The whole earth, this cold, impassive, voiceless earth,
 shall be completely justified,
Trinitas divine shall be gloriously accomplish'd and
 compacted by the true son of God, the poet,
(He shall indeed pass the straits and conquer the
 mountains,
He shall double the cape of Good Hope to some
 purpose,)
Nature and Man shall be disjoin'd and diffused no
 more,
The true son of God shall absolutely fuse them.

VI

Year at whose wide-flung door I sing!
Year of the purpose accomplish'd!
Year of the marriage of continents, climates and
 oceans!
(No mere doge of Venice now wedding the Adriatic,)
I see O year in you the vast terraqueous globe given
 and giving all,
Europe to Asia, Africa join'd, and they to the New
 World,
The lands, geographies, dancing before you, holding a
 festival garland,
As brides and bridegrooms hand in hand.

Passage to India!

Cooling airs from Caucasus far, soothing cradle of
man,

The river Euphrates flowing, the past lit up again.

Lo soul, the retrospect brought forward,

The old, most populous, wealthiest of earth's lands,

The streams of the Indus and the Ganges and their
many affluents,

(I my shores of America walking to-day behold,
resuming all,)

The tale of Alexander on his warlike marches suddenly
dying,

On one side China and on the other side Persia and
Arabia,

To the south the great seas and the bay of Bengal,

The flowing literatures, tremendous epics, religions,
castes,

Old occult Brahma interminably far back, the tender
and junior Buddha,

Central and southern empires and all their belongings,
possessors,

The wars of Tamerlane, the reign of Aurungzebe,

The traders, rulers, explorers, Moslems, Venetians,
Byzantium, the Arabs, Portuguese,

The first travelers famous yet, Marco Polo, Batouta
the Moor,

Doubts to be solv'd, the map incognita, blanks to be
    fill'd,
The foot of man unstay'd, the hands never at rest,
Thyself O soul that will not brook a challenge.

The mediæval navigators rise before me,
The world of 1492, with its awaken'd enterprise,
Something swelling in humanity now like the sap of
    the earth in spring,
The sunset splendor of chivalry declining.

And who art thou sad shade?
Gigantic, visionary, thyself a visionary,
With majestic limbs and pious beaming eyes,
Spreading around with every look of thine a golden
    world,
Enhuing it with gorgeous hues.

As the chief histrion,
Down to the footlights walks in some great scena,
Dominating the rest I see the Admiral himself,
(History's type of courage, action, faith,)
Behold him sail from Palos leading his little fleet,
His voyage behold, his return, his great fame,
His misfortunes, calumniators, behold him a prisoner,
    chain'd,
Behold his dejection, poverty, death.

(Curious in time I stand, noting the efforts of heroes,
Is the deferment long? bitter the slander, poverty,
    death?
Lies the seed unreck'd for centuries in the ground? lo,
    to God's due occasion,
Uprising in the night, it sprouts, blooms,
And fills the earth with use and beauty.)

VII

Passage indeed O soul to primal thought,
Not lands and seas alone, thy own clear freshness,
The young maturity of brood and bloom,
To realms of budding bibles.

O soul, repressless, I with thee and thou with me,
Thy circumnavigation of the world begin,
Of man, the voyage of his mind's return,
To reason's early paradise,
Back, back to wisdom's birth, to innocent intuitions,
Again with fair creation.

VIII

O we can wait no longer,
We too take ship O soul,
Joyous we too launch out on trackless seas,
Fearless for unknown shores on waves of ecstasy to
    sail,

Amid the wafting winds, (thou pressing me to thee, I
    thee to me, O soul,)
Caroling free, singing our song of God,
Chanting our chant of pleasant exploration.

With laugh and many a kiss,
(Let others deprecate, let others weep for sin, remorse,
    humiliation,)
O soul thou pleasest me, I thee.

Ah more than any priest O soul we too believe in God,
But with the mystery of God we dare not dally.

O soul thou pleasest me, I thee,
Sailing these seas or on the hills, or waking in the
    night,
Thoughts, silent thoughts, of Time and Space and
    Death, like waters flowing,
Bear me indeed as through the regions infinite,
Whose air I breathe, whose ripples hear, lave me all
    over,
Bathe me O God in thee, mounting to thee,
I and my soul to range in range of thee.

O Thou transcendent,
Nameless, the fibre and the breath,

Light of the light, shedding forth universes, thou
    centre of them,
Thou mightier centre of the true, the good, the loving,
Thou moral, spiritual fountain – affection's source –
    thou reservoir,
(O pensive soul of me – O thirst unsatisfied – waitest
    not there?
Waitest not haply for us somewhere there the
    Comrade perfect?)
Thou pulse – thou motive of the stars, suns, systems,
That, circling, move in order, safe harmonious,
Athwart the shapeless vastnesses of space,
How should I think, how breathe a single breath, how
    speak, if, out of myself,
I could not launch, to those, superior universes?

Swiftly I shrivel at the thought of God,
At Nature and its wonders, Time and Space and Death,
But that I, turning, call to thee O soul, thou actual Me,
And lo, thou gently masterest the orbs,
Thou matest Time, smilest content at Death,
And fillest, swellest full the vastnesses of Space.

Greater than stars or suns,
Bounding O soul thou journeyest forth;
What love than thine and ours could wider amplify?

What aspirations, wishes, outvie thine and ours O
    soul?
What dreams of the ideal? what plans of purity,
    perfection, strength?
What cheerful willingness for others' sake to give up
    all?
For others' sake to suffer all?

Reckoning ahead O soul, when thou, the time achiev'd,
The seas all cross'd, weather'd the capes, the voyage
    done,
Surrounded, copest, frontest God, yieldest, the aim
    attain'd,
As fill'd with friendship, love complete, the Elder
    Brother found,
The Younger melts in fondness in his arms.

IX

Passage to more than India!
Are thy wings plumed indeed for such far flights?
O soul, voyagest thou indeed on voyages like those?
Disportest thou on waters such as those?
Soundest below the Sanscrit and the Vedas?
Then have they bent unleash'd.

Passage to you, your shores, ye aged fierce enigmas!
Passage to you, to mastership of you, ye strangling
    problems!
You, strew'd with the wrecks of skeletons, that, living,
    never reach'd you.

Passage to more than India!
O secret of the earth and sky!
Of you O waters of the sea! O winding creeks and
    rivers!
Of you O woods and fields! of you strong mountains of
    my land!
Of you O prairies! of you gray rocks!
O morning red! O clouds! O rain and snows!
O day and night, passage to you!

O sun and moon and all you stars! Sirius and Jupiter!
Passage to you!

Passage, immediate passage! the blood burns in my
    veins!
Away O soul! hoist instantly the anchor!
Cut the hawsers – haul out – shake out every sail!
Have we not stood here like trees in the ground long
    enough?
Have we not grovel'd here long enough, eating and
    drinking like mere brutes?

Have we not darken'd and dazed ourselves with books
    long enough?

Sail forth – steer for the deep waters only,
Reckless O soul, exploring, I with thee, and thou with
    me,
For we are bound where mariner has not yet dared to
    go,
And we will risk the ship, ourselves and all.

O my brave soul!
O farther farther sail!
O daring joy, but safe! are they not all the seas of God?
O farther, farther, farther sail!

1871

OUT OF THE CRADLE ENDLESSLY ROCKING

Out of the cradle endlessly rocking,
Out of the mocking-bird's throat, the musical shuttle,
Out of the Ninth-month midnight,
Over the sterile sands and the fields beyond, where the
    child leaving his bed wander'd alone, bareheaded,
    barefoot,
Down from the shower'd halo,
Up from the mystic play of shadows twining and
    twisting as if they were alive,
Out from the patches of briers and blackberries,
From the memories of the bird that chanted to me,
From your memories sad brother, from the fitful
    risings and fallings I heard,
From under that yellow half-moon late-risen and
    swollen as if with tears,
From those beginning notes of yearning and love there
    in the mist,
From the thousand responses of my heart never to
    cease,
From the myriad thence-arous'd words,
From the word stronger and more delicious than any,
From such as now they start the scene revisiting,
As a flock, twittering, rising, or overhead passing,
Borne hither, ere all eludes me, hurriedly,

A man, yet by these tears a little boy again,
Throwing myself on the sand, confronting the waves,
I, chanter of pains and joys, uniter of here and
	hereafter,
Taking all hints to use them, but swiftly leaping
	beyond them,
A reminiscence sing.

Once Paumanok,
When the lilac-scent was in the air and Fifth-month
	grass was growing,
Up this seashore in some briers,
Two feather'd guests from Alabama, two together,
And their nest, and four light-green eggs spotted with
	brown,
And every day the he-bird to and fro near at hand,
And every day the she-bird crouch'd on her nest, silent,
	with bright eyes,
And every day I, a curious boy, never too close, never
	disturbing them,
Cautiously peering, absorbing, translating.

Shine! shine! shine!
Pour down your warmth, great sun!
While we bask, we two together.

Two together!
Winds blow south, or winds blow north,
Day come white, or night come black,
Home, or rivers and mountains from home,
Singing all time, minding no time,
While we two keep together.

Till of a sudden,
May-be kill'd, unknown to her mate,
One forenoon the she-bird crouch'd not on the nest,
Nor return'd that afternoon, nor the next,
Nor ever appear'd again.

And thenceforward all summer in the sound of the sea,
And at night under the full of the moon in calmer
    weather,
Over the hoarse surging of the sea,
Or flitting from brier to brier by day,
I saw, I heard at intervals the remaining one, the
    he-bird,
The solitary guest from Alabama.

Blow! blow! blow!
Blow up sea-winds along Paumanok's shore;
I wait and I wait till you blow my mate to me.

Yes, when the stars glisten'd,
All night long on the prong of a moss-scallop'd stake,
Down almost amid the slapping waves,
Sat the lone singer wonderful causing tears.

He call'd on his mate,
He pour'd forth the meanings which I of all men know.

Yes my brother I know,
The rest might not, but I have treasur'd every note,
For more than once dimly down to the beach gliding,
Silent, avoiding the moonbeams, blending myself with
     the shadows,
Recalling now the obscure shapes, the echoes, the
     sounds and sights after their sorts,
The white arms out in the breakers tirelessly tossing,
I, with bare feet, a child, the wind wafting my hair,
Listen'd long and long.

Listen'd to keep, to sing, now translating the notes,
Following you my brother.

Soothe! soothe! soothe!
Close on its wave soothes the wave behind,
And again another behind embracing and lapping, every one
  close,
But my love soothes not me, not me.

Low hangs the moon, it rose late,
It is lagging – O I think it is heavy with love, with love.

O madly the sea pushes upon the land,
With love, with love.

O night! do I not see my love fluttering out among the
  breakers?
What is that little black thing I see there in the white?

Loud! loud! loud!
Loud I call to you, my love!

High and clear I shoot my voice over the waves,
Surely you must know who is here, is here,
You must know who I am, my love.

Low-hanging moon!
What is that dusky spot in your brown yellow?
O it is the shape, the shape of my mate!
O moon do not keep her from me any longer.

Land! land! O land!
Whichever way I turn, O I think you could give me my mate
      back again if you only would,
For I am almost sure I see her dimly whichever way I look.

O rising stars!
Perhaps the one I want so much will rise, will rise with some
      of you.

O throat! O trembling throat!
Sound clearer through the atmosphere!
Pierce the woods, the earth,
Somewhere listening to catch you must be the one I want.

Shake out carols!
Solitary here, the night's carols!
Carols of lonesome love! death's carols!
Carols under that lagging, yellow, waning moon!
O under that moon where she droops almost down into the
      sea!
O reckless despairing carols.

But soft! sink low!
Soft! let me just murmur,
And do you wait a moment you husky-nois'd sea,
For somewhere I believe I heard my mate responding to me,
So faint, I must be still, be still to listen,
But not altogether still, for then she might not come
    immediately to me.

Hither my love!
Here I am! here!
With this just-sustain'd note I announce myself to you,
This gentle call is for you my love, for you.

Do not be decoy'd elsewhere,
That is the whistle of the wind, it is not my voice,
That is the fluttering, the fluttering of the spray,
Those are the shadows of leaves.

O darkness! O in vain!
O I am very sick and sorrowful.

O brown halo in the sky near the moon, drooping upon the
    sea!
O troubled reflection in the sea!
O throat! O throbbing heart!
And I singing uselessly, uselessly all the night.

O past! O happy life! O songs of joy!
In the air, in the woods, over fields,
Loved! loved! loved! loved! loved!
But my mate no more, no more with me!
We two together no more.

The aria sinking,
All else continuing, the stars shining,
The winds blowing, the notes of the bird continuous
    echoing,
With angry moans the fierce old mother incessantly
    moaning,
On the sands of Paumanok's shore gray and rustling,
The yellow half-moon enlarged, sagging down,
    drooping, the face of the sea almost touching,
The boy ecstatic, with his bare feet the waves, with his
    hair the atmosphere dallying,
The love in the heart long pent, now loose, now at last
    tumultuously bursting,
The aria's meaning, the ears, the soul, swiftly
    depositing,
The strange tears down the cheeks coursing,
The colloquy there, the trio, each uttering,
The undertone, the savage old mother incessantly
    crying,
To the boy's soul's questions sullenly timing, some
    drown'd secret hissing,
To the outsetting bard.

Demon or bird! (said the boy's soul,)
Is it indeed toward your mate you sing? or is it really
    to me?
For I, that was a child, my tongue's use sleeping, now I
    have heard you,
Now in a moment I know what I am for, I awake,
And already a thousand singers, a thousand songs,
    clearer, louder and more sorrowful than yours,
A thousand warbling echoes have started to life within
    me, never to die.

O you singer solitary, singing by yourself, projecting
    me,
O solitary me listening, never more shall I cease
    perpetuating you,
Never more shall I escape, never more the
    reverberations,
Never more the cries of unsatisfied love be absent from
    me,
Never again leave me to be the peaceful child I was
    before what there in the night,
By the sea under the yellow and sagging moon,
The messenger there arous'd, the fire, the sweet hell
    within,
The unknown want, the destiny of me.

O give me the clew! (it lurks in the night here
    somewhere,)
O if I am to have so much, let me have more!

A word then, (for I will conquer it,)
The word final, superior to all,
Subtle, sent up – what is it? – I listen;
Are you whispering it, and have been all the time, you
    sea-waves?
Is that it from your liquid rims and wet sands?

Whereto answering, the sea,
Delaying not, hurrying not,
Whisper'd me through the night, and very plainly
    before daybreak,
Lisp'd to me the low and delicious word death,
And again death, death, death, death,
Hissing melodious, neither like the bird nor like my
    arous'd child's heart,
But edging near as privately for me rustling at my feet,
Creeping thence steadily up to my ears and laving me
    softly all over,
Death, death, death, death, death.

Which I do not forget,
But fuse the song of my dusky demon and brother,
That he sang to me in the moonlight on Paumanok's
    gray beach,
With the thousand responsive songs at random,
My own songs awaked from that hour,
And with them the key, the word up from the waves,
The word of the sweetest song and all songs,
That strong and delicious word which, creeping to my
    feet,
(Or like some old crone rocking the cradle, swathed in
    sweet garments, bending aside,)
The sea whisper'd me.

1859

WHEN LILACS LAST IN THE DOORYARD BLOOM'D

I

When lilacs last in the dooryard bloom'd,
And the great star early droop'd in the western sky in
the night,
I mourn'd, and yet shall mourn with ever-returning
spring.

Ever-returning spring, trinity sure to me you bring,
Lilac blooming perennial and drooping star in the
west,
And thought of him I love.

II

O powerful western fallen star!
O shades of night – O moody, tearful night!
O great star disappear'd – O the black murk that hides
the star!
O cruel hands that hold me powerless – O helpless soul
of me!
O harsh surrounding cloud that will not free my soul.

III

In the dooryard fronting an old farm-house near the
      white-wash'd palings,
Stands the lilac-bush tall-growing with heart-shaped
      leaves of rich green,
With many a pointed blossom rising delicate, with the
      perfume strong I love,
With every leaf a miracle – and from this bush in the
      dooryard,
With delicate-color'd blossoms and heart-shaped
      leaves of rich green,
A sprig with its flower I break.

IV

In the swamp in secluded recesses,
A shy and hidden bird is warbling a song.

Solitary the thrush,
The hermit withdrawn to himself, avoiding the
      settlements,
Sings by himself a song.

Song of the bleeding throat,
Death's outlet song of life, (for well dear brother I
      know,
If thou wast not granted to sing thou would'st surely
      die.)

V

Over the breast of the spring, the land, amid cities,
Amid lanes and through old woods, where lately the
    violets peep'd from the ground, spotting the gray
    debris,
Amid the grass in the fields each side of the lanes,
    passing the endless grass,
Passing the yellow-spear'd wheat, every grain from its
    shroud in the dark-brown fields uprisen,
Passing the apple-tree blows of white and pink in the
    orchards,
Carrying a corpse to where it shall rest in the grave,
Night and day journeys a coffin.

VI

Coffin that passes through lanes and streets,
Through day and night with the great cloud darkening
    the land,
With the pomp of the inloop'd flags with the cities
    draped in black,
With the show of the States themselves as of crape-
    veil'd women standing,
With processions long and winding and the flambeaus
    of the night,
With the countless torches lit, with the silent sea of
    faces and the unbared heads,

With the waiting depot, the arriving coffin, and the
     sombre faces,
With dirges through the night, with the thousand
     voices rising strong and solemn,
With all the mournful voices of the dirges pour'd
     around the coffin,
The dim-lit churches and the shuddering organs –
     where amid these you journey,
With the tolling tolling bells' perpetual clang,
Here, coffin that slowly passes,
I give you my sprig of lilac.

VII

(Nor for you, for one alone,
Blossoms and branches green to coffins all I bring,
For fresh as the morning, thus would I chant a song for
     you O sane and sacred death.

All over bouquets of roses,
O death, I cover you over with roses and early lilies,
But mostly and now the lilac that blooms the first,
Copious I break, I break the sprigs from the bushes,
With loaded arms I come, pouring for you,
For you and the coffins all of you O death.)

VIII

O western orb sailing the heaven,
Now I know what you must have meant as a month
      since I walk'd,
As I walk'd in silence the transparent shadowy night,
As I saw you had something to tell as you bent to me
      night after night,
As you droop'd from the sky low down as if to my side,
      (while the other stars all look'd on,)
As we wander'd together the solemn night, (for
      something I know not what kept me from sleep,)
As the night advanced, and I saw on the rim of the
      west how full you were of woe,
As I stood on the rising ground in the breeze in the
      cool transparent night,
As I watch'd where you pass'd and was lost in the
      netherward black of the night,
As my soul in its trouble dissatisfied sank, as where
      you sad orb,
Concluded, dropt in the night, and was gone.

IX

Sing on there in the swamp,
O singer bashful and tender, I hear your notes, I hear
      your call,
I hear, I come presently, I understand you,

But a moment I linger, for the lustrous star has
    detain'd me,
The star my departing comrade holds and detains me.

X

O how shall I warble myself for the dead one there I
    loved?
And how shall I deck my song for the large sweet soul
    that has gone?
And what shall my perfume be for the grave of him I
    love?

Sea-winds blown from east and west,
Blown from the Eastern sea and blown from the
    Western sea, till there on the prairies meeting,
These and with these and the breath of my chant,
I'll perfume the grave of him I love.

XI

O what shall I hang on the chamber walls?
And what shall the pictures be that I hang on the walls,
To adorn the burial-house of him I love?

Pictures of growing spring and farms and homes,
With the Fourth-month eve at sundown, and the gray
    smoke lucid and bright,

With floods of the yellow gold of the gorgeous,
    indolent, sinking sun, burning, expanding the air,
With the fresh sweet herbage under foot, and the pale
    green leaves of the trees prolific,
In the distance the flowing glaze, the breast of the
    river, with a wind-dapple here and there,
With ranging hills on the banks, with many a line
    against the sky, and shadows,
And the city at hand with dwellings so dense, and
    stacks of chimneys,
And all the scenes of life and the workshops, and the
    workmen homeward returning.

XII

Lo, body and soul – this land,
My own Manhattan with spires, and the sparkling and
    hurrying tides, and the ships,
The varied and ample land, the South and the North in
    the light, Ohio's shores and flashing Missouri,
And ever the far-spreading prairies cover'd with grass
    and corn.

Lo, the most excellent sun so calm and haughty,
The violet and purple morn with just-felt breezes,
The gentle soft-born measureless light,
The miracle spreading bathing all, the fulfill'd noon,

The coming eve delicious, the welcome night and the
     stars,
Over my cities shining all, enveloping man and land.

XIII

Sing on, sing on you gray-brown bird,
Sing from the swamps, the recesses, pour your chant
     from the bushes,
Limitless out of the dusk, out of the cedars and pines.

Sing on dearest brother, warble your reedy song,
Loud human song, with voice of uttermost woe.

O liquid and free and tender!
O wild and loose to my soul – O wondrous singer!
You only I hear – yet the star holds me, (but will soon
     depart,)
Yet the lilac with mastering odor holds me.

XIV

Now while I sat in the day and look'd forth,
In the close of the day with its light and the fields of
     spring, and the farmers preparing their crops,
In the large unconscious scenery of my land with its
     lakes and forests,
In the heavenly aerial beauty, (after the perturb'd
     winds and the storms,)

Under the arching heavens of the afternoon swift
 passing, and the voices of children and women,
The many-moving sea-tides, and I saw the ships how
 they sail'd,
And the summer approaching with richness, and the
 fields all busy with labor,
And the infinite separate houses, how they all went on,
 each with its meals and minutia of daily usages,
And the streets how their throbbings throbb'd, and the
 cities pent – lo, then and there,
Falling upon them all and among them all, enveloping
 me with the rest,
Appear'd the cloud, appear'd the long black trail,
And I knew death, its thought, and the sacred
 knowledge of death.

Then with the knowledge of death as walking one side
 of me,
And the thought of death close-walking the other side
 of me,
And I in the middle as with companions, and as
 holding the hands of companions,
I fled forth to the hiding receiving night that talks not,
Down to the shores of the water, the path by the
 swamp in the dimness,
To the solemn shadowy cedars and ghostly pines so
 still.

And the singer so shy to the rest receiv'd me,
The gray-brown bird I know receiv'd us comrades
    three,
And he sang the carol of death, and a verse for him I
    love.

From deep secluded recesses,
From the fragrant cedars and the ghostly pines so still,
Came the carol of the bird.

And the charm of the carol rapt me,
As I held as if by their hands my comrades in the night,
And the voice of my spirit tallied the song of the bird.

Come lovely and soothing death,
Undulate round the world, serenely arriving, arriving,
In the day, in the night, to all, to each,
Sooner or later delicate death.

Prais'd be the fathomless universe,
For life and joy, and for objects and knowledge curious,
And for love, sweet love — but praise! praise! praise!
For the sure-enwinding arms of cool-enfolding death.

Dark mother always gliding near with soft feet,
Have none chanted for thee a chant of fullest welcome?
Then I chant it for thee, I glorify thee above all,
I bring thee a song that when thou must indeed come, come
    unfalteringly.

Approach strong deliveress,
When it is so, when thou hast taken them I joyously sing the
    dead,
Lost in the loving floating ocean of thee,
Laved in the flood of thy bliss O death.

From me to thee glad serenades,
Dances for thee I propose saluting thee, adornments and
    feastings for thee,
And the sights of the open landscape and the high-spread sky
    are fitting,
And life and the fields, and the huge and thoughtful night.

The night in silence under many a star,
The ocean shore and the husky whispering wave whose voice
    I know,
And the soul turning to thee O vast and well-veil'd death,
And the body gratefully nestling close to thee.

Over the tree-tops I float thee a song,
Over the rising and sinking waves, over the myriad fields
and the prairies wide,
Over the dense-pack'd cities all and the teeming wharves
and ways,
I float this carol with joy, with joy to thee O death.

XV

To the tally of my soul,
Loud and strong kept up the gray-brown bird,
With pure deliberate notes spreading filling the night.

Loud in the pines and cedars dim,
Clear in the freshness moist and the swamp-perfume,
And I with my comrades there in the night.

While my sight that was bound in my eyes unclosed,
As to long panoramas of visions.

And I saw askant the armies,
I saw as in noiseless dreams hundreds of battle-flags,
Borne through the smoke of the battles and pierc'd
    with missiles I saw them,
And carried hither and yon through the smoke, and
    torn and bloody,
And at last but a few shreds left on the staffs, (and all in
    silence,)
And the staffs all splinter'd and broken.

I saw battle-corpses, myriads of them,
And the white skeletons of young men, I saw them,
I saw the debris and debris of all the slain soldiers of
    the war,
But I saw they were not as was thought,
They themselves were fully at rest, they suffer'd not,
The living remain'd and suffer'd, the mother suffer'd,
And the wife and the child and the musing comrade
    suffer'd,
And the armies that remain'd suffer'd.

XVI

Passing the visions, passing the night,
Passing, unloosing the hold of my comrades' hands,
Passing the song of the hermit bird and the tallying
    song of my soul,
Victorious song, death's outlet song, yet varying ever-
    altering song,
As low and wailing, yet clear the notes, rising and
    falling, flooding the night,
Sadly sinking and fainting, as warning and warning,
    and yet again bursting with joy,
Covering the earth and filling the spread of the heaven,
As that powerful psalm in the night I heard from
    recesses,
Passing, I leave thee lilac with heart-shaped leaves,
I leave thee there in the door-yard, blooming,
    returning with spring.

I cease from my song for thee,
From my gaze on thee in the west, fronting the west,
    communing with thee,
O comrade lustrous with silver face in the night.

Yet each to keep and all, retrievements out of the
    night,
The song, the wondrous chant of the gray-brown bird,
And the tallying chant, the echo arous'd in my soul,
With the lustrous and drooping star with the
    countenance full of woe,
With the holders holding my hand nearing the call of
    the bird,
Comrades mine and I in the midst, and their memory
    ever to keep, for the dead I loved so well,
For the sweetest, wisest soul of all my days and lands —
    and this for his dear sake,
Lilac and star and bird twined with the chant of my
    soul,
There in the fragrant pines and the cedars dusk and
    dim.

1865—6

WHISPERS OF HEAVENLY DEATH

Whispers of heavenly death murmur'd I hear,
Labial gossip of night, sibilant chorals,
Footsteps gently ascending, mystical breezes wafted
    soft and low,
Ripples of unseen rivers, tides of a current flowing,
    forever flowing,
(Or is it the plashing of tears? the measureless waters
    of human tears?)

I see, just see skyward, great cloud-masses,
Mournfully slowly they roll, silently swelling and
    mixing,
With at times a half-dimm'd sadden'd far-off star,
Appearing and disappearing.

(Some parturition rather, some solemn immortal birth;
On the frontiers to eyes impenetrable,
Some soul is passing over.)

1868

SO LONG!

To conclude, I announce what comes after me.

I remember I said before my leaves sprang at all,
I would raise my voice jocund and strong with
      reference to consummations.

When America does what was promis'd,
When through these States walk a hundred millions of
      superb persons,
When the rest part away for superb persons and
      contribute to them,
When breeds of the most perfect mothers denote
      America,
Then to me and mine our due fruition.

I have press'd through in my own right,
I have sung the body and the soul, war and peace have I
      sung, and the songs of life and death,
And the songs of birth, and shown that there are many
      births.

I have offer'd my style to every one, I have journey'd
      with confident step;
While my pleasure is yet at the full I whisper *So long!*
And take the young woman's hand and the young
      man's hand for the last time.

I announce natural persons to arise,
I announce justice triumphant,
I announce uncompromising liberty and equality,
I announce the justification of candor and the
     justification of pride.

I announce that the identity of these States is a single
     identity only,
I announce the Union more and more compact,
     indissoluble,
I announce splendors and majesties to make all the
     previous politics of the earth insignificant.

I announce adhesiveness, I say it shall be limitless,
     unloosen'd,
I say you shall yet find the friend you were looking for.

I announce a man or woman coming, perhaps you are
     the one, (*So long!*)
I announce the great individual, fluid as Nature, chaste,
     affectionate, compassionate, fully arm'd.

I announce a life that shall be copious, vehement,
     spiritual, bold,
I announce an end that shall lightly and joyfully meet
     its translation.

I announce myriads of youths, beautiful, gigantic,
   sweet-blooded,
I announce a race of splendid and savage old men.

O thicker and faster – (*So long!*)
O crowding too close upon me,
I foresee too much, it means more than I thought,
It appears to me I am dying.

Hasten throat and sound your last,
Salute me – salute the days once more. Peal the old cry
   once more.

Screaming electric, the atmosphere using,
At random glancing, each as I notice absorbing,
Swiftly on, but a little while alighting,
Curious envelop'd messages delivering,
Sparkles hot, seed ethereal down in the dirt dropping,
Myself unknowing, my commission obeying, to
   question it never daring,
To ages and ages yet the growth of the seed leaving,
To troops out of the war arising, they the tasks I have
   set promulging,
To women certain whispers of myself bequeathing,
   their affection me more clearly explaining,
To young men my problems offering – no dallier I –
   I the muscle of their brains trying,
So I pass, a little time vocal, visible, contrary,

Afterwards a melodious echo, passionately bent for,
     (death making me really undying,)
The best of me then when no longer visible, for toward
     that I have been incessantly preparing.

What is there more, that I lag and pause and crouch
     extended with unshut mouth?
Is there a single final farewell?

My songs cease, I abandon them,
From behind the screen where I hid I advance
     personally solely to you.

Camerado, this is no book,
Who touches this touches a man,
(Is it night? are we here together alone?)
It is I you hold and who holds you,
I spring from the pages into your arms – decease calls
     me forth.

O how your fingers drowse me,
Your breath falls around me like dew, your pulse lulls
     the tympans of my ears,
I feel immerged from head to foot,
Delicious, enough.

Enough O deed impromptu and secret,
Enough O gliding present – enough O summ'd-up
    past.

Dear friend whoever you are take this kiss,
I give it especially to you, do not forget me,
I feel like one who has done work for the day to retire
    awhile,
I receive now again of my many translations, from my
    avataras ascending, while others doubtless await
    me,
An unknown sphere more real than I dream'd, more
    direct, darts awakening rays about me, *So long!*
Remember my words, I may again return,
I love you, I depart from materials,
I am as one disembodied, triumphant, dead.

1860

INDEX OF FIRST LINES

A glimpse through an interstice caught   20

A line in long array where they wind betwixt
green   43

A noiseless patient spider   23

A sight in camp in the daybreak gray and dim   37

Among the men and women the multitude   21

An old man bending I come among new faces   44

As I lay with my head in your lap camerado   50

As I sit in twilight late alone by the flickering oak   30

Come said the Muse   11

Far back, related on my mother's side   29

Flood-tide below me! I see you face to face!   51

Hold it up sternly – see this it sends back   26

I celebrate myself, and sing myself   87

I hear America singing, the varied carols I hear ..   13

In a little house keep I pictures suspended, it is
not a   25

I saw in Louisiana a live-oak growing   18

I wander all night in my vision   186

Me imperturbe, standing at ease in Nature   24

Native moments – when you come upon me – ah
you   14

Not from successful love alone   27

On a flat road runs the well-train'd runner   32

Only themselves understand themselves and the
like of   32

O tan-faced prairie-boy 33

Out of the cradle endlessly rocking 219

Passing stranger! you do not know how longingly
I 19

Poets to come! orators, singers, musicians to come! 12

Roots and leaves themselves alone are these 17

Singing my days 203

Skirting the river road, (my forenoon walk, my
rest,) 28

Sometimes with one I love I fill myself with rage
for 33

Starting from fish-shape Paumanok where I was
born 66

There was a child went forth every day 62

These carols sung to cheer my passage through
the 11

To conclude, I announce what comes after me 245

Vigil strange I kept on the field one night 39

When I heard at the close of the day how my
name had 15

When lilacs last in the dooryard bloom'd 230

Whispers of heavenly death murmur'd I hear 244

Whoever you are holding me now in hand 34

With its cloud of skirmishers in advance 42

Word over all, beautiful as the sky 49

Youth, large, lusty, loving – youth full of grace,
force 22